WHY WE ARE WHO WE ARE

By the Same Author

Living Spirituality

To the Beginning of the End of Karma

WHY WE ARE WHO WE ARE

An Insightful Glimpse into Our Human Roles, Soul Personality, and Karmic Mandates

MEETU BISHT

HAY HOUSE INDIA

New Delhi • London • Sydney
Carlsbad, California • New York City

Hay House Publishers (India) Pvt Ltd
Muskaan Complex, Plot No. 3, B-2, Vasant Kunj, New Delhi – 110070, India

Hay House LLC, P.O. Box 5100, Carlsbad, CA 92018-5100, USA
Hay House UK Ltd, 1st Floor, Crawford Corner, 91-93 Baker Street, London W1U 6QQ, UK
Hay House Australia Publishing Pty Ltd, 18/36 Ralph St., Alexandria NSW 2015, Australia

Email: contact@hayhouse.co.in
Website: www.hayhouse.co.in

First published by Hay House India, 2023
Reprint, 2026
18 17 16 15 14 13 12 11 10 9

ISBN 978-93-94613-94-2
ISBN 978-93-94613-86-7 (ebook)

Printed at Replika Press Pvt Ltd

MIX
Paper | Supporting responsible forestry
FSC www.fsc.org FSC™ C016779

Hay House is committed to a sustainable future for our business, our readers and our planet. This book is made from Forest Stewardship Council® certified paper.

To the Source Energy—the Supreme Soul
whose love, inspiration, and guidance resulted
in this effort.
I dedicate this book to you!

Contents

PREFACE

Every book has its own destiny and its own unique timing, which is, sometimes, even unknown to the authors who bring it out into the world. I say so because this is a book, that I didn't quite intend on writing. But while I was working on another book, I found that two different books had unintentionally taken shape. And the first one of the two is *Why We Are Who We Are*.

Why We Are Who We Are talks about the various roles souls play in their form-based reality, the karmic mandates attached to these roles, and the ways one can make better sense of the self in reference to these roles as well as their karmic obligations. The book also sheds light on the very purpose of our individual journeys, which for each soul, varies and is based on their individual balance of karmas and their state of spiritual evolution.

For me, it was important to write this book as during the last seven years, I encountered a strange commonality in my interactions that made me understand the largely biased perceptions and the deeply conditioned state of human beings which is the very cause of their confusion and suffering. It keeps them unaware of the fact that whatever one experiences or encounters in life is a response to their inner being and that it's one's tendencies and soul personality which create the situations that one needs to deal with by paying greater attention to the self.

Hence, this book endeavours to clear the confusion around our inner being, tendencies, soul personality, karmic mandates, and individual roles that we play in this human journey. It's relevant for people who are keen to change, grow, and operate through higher consciousness as well as for those who question their given roles, complain, or remain stressed about life and judge the creator as being unfair. Most importantly, the book will enable the reader to understand the self and their spiritual reality, or, in other words, realise why we are who we are.

INTRODUCTION

We are souls and we are on a journey . . . a long journey that has made us who we are and that holds the promise of what we can be. And though it is possible to understand who we are, how we are, and our inner reality, most of us do not seek this knowledge and remain unaware of these aspects of our lives.

The fact is that we can be a lot more than what we are today, if only we understand and relate to the truth behind why we are and who we are as souls, as personalities, as people, and as human beings. This book is an attempt to decode our deeper mystery and demystify the enigma of our spiritual state and evolution, which is the very basis of our human life and destiny. It is an attempt to both spiritually and logically realise what makes us who we are, the reason behind our unique and explicit human roles, and how we can ascend or evolve as souls through this mortal journey.

SECTION 1

The first section of this book provides a broad perspective on certain key factors such as soul personality, tendencies, and karma that lay the foundation of who we are and the life we live. It explains the deep correlation between our soul personality and the roles we acquire in our human form. Here, we also talk about the real purpose of life, what makes life what it is, and how we are solely responsible for the nature of our individual lives and our state of being.

This section also uncovers the true objective of our human roles and explains why we need to play these roles well and how we can achieve inner maturity, growth, personality refinement, and evolution. It also touches upon the relevance of past lives in deciding our present life reality and how the universe assists us by giving us the role that supports our higher purpose.

All in all, this section explores the fundamentals that help decode the mystery behind our distinct lives and the individual journeys we undertake in this human form. It briefly touches upon the ways in which we can harmonise with our human role in order to achieve its key objective.

Chapter 1

LIFE IS NOT WHAT WE THINK IT IS

As much as we would like to believe that we are here for some worldly goals, pursuits, gains, joys, gratification, celebrations, etc., the fact is that it is not true. As much as we would like to believe that we are here to pursue external things, such as work, relationships, name, culture, religion, a home, family, marriage, career, money, achievements, friendship, entertainment, indulgence, adventure, faith, rituals, geographies, etc., the fact is that our potential is much more. As much as we would like to believe that our individual life amounts to just our duties, responsibilities, ambition, goals, celebrations, pain, and pleasure, the fact is that there is more to life. And as much as we would like to believe that our life is built outside of us, the fact is that it's all within us.

The truth is that life is not about what we have or what we own individually. Rather, it is about the person that we are deep within while dealing with this everyday process of existence and survival. Life is also not about accumulating worldly or material things but about our response to everything that we accumulate—our experiences, battles, glories, challenges, triumphs, and defeats. And most of all, life is the person we become in the process.

Thus, our life cannot be defined by labels or be graded on the basis of material accumulations and achievements or the lack of them. Our life is who we are as individuals or as consciousness disguised in a physical form. It is also about how or what we feel about the self.

In the absolute sense, our life is defined by our tendencies, our thoughts, our perceptions, our feelings, and our deepest state of being. In other words, our life is nothing but a reflection of the quality of our energy, the state of our consciousness, and the colour of our individual souls. Therefore, what we are within radiates as our life outside.

The next thing to understand is that if our life is a reflection of what we are as an individual, then what are the factors that go into making who we are? The primary factors that shape us include what we have encountered externally and how we have dealt with it internally. Basically, our personality is defined by all our emotions, feelings, karmic imprints, and tendencies combined together.

For example, a person may enjoy all the affluence of this world and have everything worldly marked as perfect and yet, they can be oversensitive, anxious, disturbed, and even depressed. After all, have we not seen even the most accomplished people combat mental agony or dwell in emotionally difficult states? Among such people, there also have been a few who have succumbed to perpetual misery or even gone to the extent of putting an untimely end to their lives. And given this scenario, what really does their life amount to? Do their achievements on a worldly scale really matter? Can their life be defined as successful or happy or good? And with them being at constant war with their emotions, does the glamour and triumph of their external world really add any value and meaning to their life?

The answer is no! For it does not really matter how one physically lives in this world or what one achieves in this world as material success, fame, and recognition. What truly matters is how one leaves, or more specifically, what is one's state of mind or one's level of consciousness at the end of this finite human journey. That truly amounts to one's entire life. This is the highest goal that we as humans can aspire for.

So, we can see that life is not about what happens to us; it is about what we become as a result or in response to the events and experiences that we come across in due course of our individual journeys. Therefore, it becomes extremely important to:

- Understand and accept the true context of life.
- Realise early that whatever we hold within is what our life will eventually amount to.
- Accept the fact that our life is our own making regardless of our experiences, situations, and relationships. It is only we as individuals that decide or define the quality of our own life.

Remember that this human form that has been given to us is meant to strengthen us, heal us, transform us, and lift us to a higher energy! It has been given to us so that we get a rational understanding of the self and handle the self with greater attention and care. Hence, our birth is perhaps the greatest opportunity in our journey as a being or a soul. One can do so much with it in terms of becoming a higher and more elevated being.

But then again, we can live for a hundred years and still not realise why we are here. We may still not understand what makes life and as a result, not know why we are who we are. It all depends on the effort we put in to know the true meaning and purpose of this life and the sincerity we show in understanding the self . . . our deepest and most real self!

Chapter 2
KNOWING THE SELF

To know the self, we need to relate to the self not as the body but as a being or a soul. This being is the real driving force that determines everything from one's personality to behaviour to choices and even the experiences that one goes through in life.

Thinking of the self as the body results in not just one but many other false identifications. Like identification with a name, family, culture, religion, society, certain geography, designation, role, and so much more, that may be a part of us but do not amount to the real self! Yet, we get so consumed with these various identifications that we permanently start seeking life outside of us. And if we do not become aware of this fact, each of these aspects can take over our mind and our entire life!

Therefore, on this journey to greater self-awareness, the first thing that is required is to have the right reference with regard to the self. This process becomes easier once we begin to participate in deeper reflections, associate with some form of higher wisdom and spiritual knowledge, learn to silence all the noise and chatter of the mind, and spend more time in deep contemplation of the self. It is in such moments that we may feel the body to be different from our true being and relate to that dimension within us, which is the real force behind everything that defines our life.

A major opposition on this path of self-realisation is posed by our conditioning, which is a result of having lived countless lifetimes as a body, as a name, as a culture, and as any other label in the world of forms. Such conditioning is not easy to break, as these patterns of false identifications become habitual and deeply imbibed over an indefinable time. Also, most of us prefer being constantly trapped in a box of limited mindsets and restricted beliefs as stepping out of it seem like a direct threat to our false sense of security. This is why so many people dismiss the idea of self-realisation as unnecessary and give up before they reach their goal.

Another reason why altering our conditioning is not that simple or easy is because once we become accustomed to running after physical pleasures and a sense of gratification which comes through material things and worldly relationships, we will find making any effort to know the true self becomes somewhat uninteresting. But at any given point, if we aim to seek greater self-awareness, the foremost thing that we must establish and comprehend is our true identity. We must make the effort to understand that this body, which we believe to be who we really are, is just a vehicle that carries us from one end to another. Also, we must realise that on this entire journey, what we gather is a whole lot of impressions (karma) and tendencies that prepare us or rather qualify us for yet another role, in yet another lifetime. After all, the body cannot pull along forever!

Thus, we can see that what we gather through our journey from infancy to the end is nothing but our soul's quality or personality. And it is on basis of this quality/personality that we get another physical form, another birth, our next set of circumstances, family, society, culture, destiny, and life experiences. We can say that our life on earth is akin to attending a school where we acquire wisdom, learn, evolve, and grow. And even though the school, curriculum, teachers, environment, experiences, etc., all play a vital role in shaping what we eventually become, they are just temporary features in our lives. Similarly, when we enter a particular lifetime, we experience certain kinds of interactions and environments, which go on to shape the person that we become. And it is this person, which can also be called the being or soul with its accumulated tendencies, that remains even when everything else ends or transforms, as we move from one lifetime to another.

The important thing to realise here is that we are all coming from someplace and some life into the present one. The fact that even babies have distinctive personalities and that we are all born in different circumstances to different destinies, different life paths, and different environments goes on to prove that something is being carried forward from our previous births. This can be further seen in the cases of twins as even they do not have similar destinies or similar traits, as well as in cases where children are radically different from their parents and their lineage. This again confirms that something comes with us when we enter a life and on the basis of which, we get what we do and become who we are.

The point to note here is that this 'something' reveals the most significant truth of life—that we are souls on a journey spanning innumerable lifetimes and that we are not this body, and instead, we are only experiencing this world through the body. And this is the most fundamental identification that we need in order to progress on our path to greater self-awareness, higher consciousness, and an empowered state of being. But until we familiarise the mind with the real self and partially withdraw from physical identifications and labels, we will not understand the significance of why we need to evolve as a being. We will not feel the necessity to devote time to the self and invest in building soul power. Not only that, but if we fail to make the correct identification, there is every chance that we will keep fighting our inner demons (ego, anger, anxiety, greed, attachments, lust, etc.) birth after birth. We will not be able to address anything negative or difficult in life, and not achieve the true purpose of our physical existence, which is peace and enlightenment. It is a fact that a lack of true identity is often the reason behind all the chaos in our minds today and why we feel tired and easily succumb to boredom, stress, hurt, depression, anger, and pain. And the same is like fighting our battles in darkness, not knowing where we are aiming our arrows and from where we are getting struck.

Hence, correctly identifying with the true self is unquestionably a vital prerequisite to leading a happy and fulfilling life. A life from which we carry our emotional and psychological memories that transcend many births. So, always remember that we are entities beyond this body, we are energy in motion, and we are here in this transactional world to reach our higher selves.

Chapter 3

SOUL, KARMA, TENDENCIES, AND EVOLUTION

'Why was I born?'

Most of us would ask this question at some point in our lives. Perhaps, while sitting alone and sipping a hot beverage, or when the hectic pace and uncertainty of life get on our nerves, we wonder why things are happening the way they are. And even if this inadvertent self-analysis is rather momentary—because we seldom have time or the inclination to delve into the deeper questions of life—one thing is certain that at some definite point in our lives, we will be curious to know about the reason why we take birth and why we leave!

The fact of the matter is that whether or not we want to unravel this truth or, let us say, whether or not this all-important question pops up in our head, be sure that it is extremely important for all of us to know the reason behind our birth and the significance of death and rebirth. For only when we know and understand why we are here, what we take with us when we die, and what really comes back with us through another birth, only then will we feel the necessity to evolve as a being and dedicate some part of our time to the real purpose of our human life, which is spiritual growth and evolution. Until then, we will keep grappling with life with a sense of cluelessness and exasperation.

So, once we get a sense of our true identity and are able to relate to the self as a soul, the next imperative thing is to assess the following questions:

- What exactly is the real purpose of this journey?
- What are we likely to gather in a given lifespan as souls?
- What is it that will persist even after death and how will it affect us?

These are important questions that we need to ask and contemplate. And as we search for a common thread that runs through all the above questions, the four keywords that come to the surface are:

1. Soul
2. Karma
3. Tendencies
4. Evolution

These are four of the most significant features of human life that demand greater understanding and analysis! Therefore, let us explore them a bit deeper.

Soul

Soul is energy that inhabits human form and gives it life. It is the driving force of life in humans and is the non-physical entity in the physical. It is also the seat of human thoughts, feelings, and emotions. Hence, the soul is the controller of the body and it enters this cycle of birth and death when it has to get into an exchange of energy with the world of forms.

The soul can also be understood as consciousness that is eternal. So, even after the body gives up or as consciousness exits the body, it remains as it transcends forms. This consciousness experiences life and creates impressions which determine its higher or lower states. It then carries these impressions, also known as tendencies and karma, from one life to another.

Karma

A body enables a soul to experience the world, but more importantly, it brings the soul into the field of karma. And what is karma?

Karma is the outcome of the exchange of energy with the world of forms. It is the combined effect of one's intentions, thoughts, words, emotions, and actions, along with their consequences, all put together. These aspects essentially execute and govern all the interactions and energy exchanges that a soul experiences through its time in a human form. These aspects also get coded as patterns within the framework of the soul and play a significant role in the human journey of the soul.

And there really is no escape from karma. Once born as a human, one will have to participate in life through *karm* (action or deeds) and this will result into karma (the energy of those deeds). In fact, karma is the reason why we are born and karma is the reason why we leave this world. Our birth is an opportunity to dissolve old patterns of karma (thoughts, words, intentions, actions, and emotions), though in the process we are also likely to build new patterns that become the very basis of our journey ahead in future lifetimes.

Tendencies

Then there are tendencies that combine into a soul's personality! There are positive tendencies such as peace, love, happiness, goodness, warmth, compassion, optimism, humility, kindness, etc., and then there are negative tendencies such as anger, jealousy, hate, pride, ego, hurt, fear, greed, etc.

A soul brings with it certain tendencies, both good and bad, from its former lifetimes and is again bound to gather, cultivate, and even dissolve certain tendencies in its present lifetime.

And how does a soul do the same? Through karm, of course! For once a soul begins to perform action or deeds (karm), there will be an exchange of energy with the world of forms and every interaction and exchange of intentions, thoughts, words, emotions, and actions with other people or with various situations leaves an impression on the soul. This impression is termed karma. And depending upon the quality of the energy exchange or the quality of karma, a soul, after repeated impressions, gathers a certain tendency.

Therefore, positive energy exchanges help a soul gather positive tendencies, dissolve old, negative tendencies, and even further strengthen its existing positive tendencies. However, when a soul experiences or performs negative karma (negative energy exchanges), it accumulates certain negative tendencies and also empowers what is already not right in its personality. Negative karma creates impressions like fear, anger, guilt, sorrow, and hurt. And these impressions eventually convert into tendencies that become a part of a soul's active nature. And when these tendencies become a soul's active nature or personality, its original nature of love, peace, and happiness becomes dormant, resulting in a loss of powers. This loss of power also makes the soul accumulate more karmic debts.

So, we could also say that tendencies and karma share a symbiotic relationship. Meaning, the type of karmic pattern will be determined by the specific tendencies of the soul.

Also, a more pronounced karmic pattern will play a greater role in shaping a soul's tendencies.

Evolution

The most important aspect of a soul's journey through a human life is its evolution. Primarily because it is for the sake of evolution that a soul is born. It is for the sake of ascending in power and purity that a soul is born. It is born to regain what has been lost—its virtues and inherent powers—over repeated births. It is born to enhance its positive tendencies and eliminate the negative ones in its personality, so that it can evolve to a higher life and perhaps, understand its bigger role in the scheme of the universe. A role which may present itself on the material plane or in some higher dimension. No one can tell when will this role appear but it always does. As the very purpose of human birth is to help the soul ascend to its higher self. This ascension is the ultimate incentive that drives every soul towards evolution and growth and gives a higher purpose to human life. No wonder then that being born is the greatest opportunity for a soul.

This brings us to the next important question: How does the soul get to evolve?

A soul can evolve by creating the right kind of karmas and by empowering the self with the correct set of tendencies, which, during the course of a lifetime, can be achieved by paying the necessary attention to the self, by living with greater self-awareness, and by working on the self as long as the physical form exists! And only when we dedicate some bit of our life and our precious time to understanding the self, assessing the self, talking to the self, discovering more about the self, and feeding the self with the right information and higher wisdom, can we become capable of enhancing the self deep within, which, in turn, will propagate our evolution as a soul.

But if we don't evolve as a soul, we will keep going around in circles and not achieve the real purpose of our birth. We will also stay perplexed about life and won't ever find real solutions to our troubles! Most importantly, by not rising to a higher consciousness, we will further reduce our soul power. This can be highly detrimental to our prospects in this material plane because this loss of soul power inadvertently strengthens the ego, which is the root of all our troubles. And if we continue to lose our spiritual powers/our soul's strength, owing to wrong references to life as well as the self, we would end up experiencing some really turbulent lifetimes. This is because when we keep living in oblivion and self-denial, life throws difficult situations at us so that we wake up and seek the mandatory wisdom to become self-aware.

So, if a soul loses its powers over the course of its various births, the only way to regain them is by achieving self-awareness and by making the necessary effort to rise to its higher self through higher wisdom. And this switch from a disempowered state to an empowered state is what every soul gets to experience at different levels and at different speeds and upon this transition depends its eventual evolution and growth. This is the reason why working on the self is of utmost significance. It not only helps us gather positive tendencies but also helps eliminate and dissolve the aspects of our soul's personality that make us weak and disempowered. It also helps us attract positive life experiences and regain our lost powers.

Our tendencies are of utmost importance because they are the primary cause of every karma we create. And tendencies together with karma define the quality of a soul and enhancing this quality with every birth is evolution.

Chapter 4
BALANCING SOUL PERSONALITY

Whether it is past life regression or the theory of reincarnation, they all reveal to us that we all have played different parts in different human forms through different lifetimes. And through these different lifetimes, we have essayed various roles and genders that have led to an accumulation of tendencies, predominantly in our soul personality. Hence, it does not really matter who we are born as in the present birth; what matters is that we realise why we are born a certain gender and type.

Through the entire cycle of birth, death, and rebirth, the universe aims to balance our soul personality. Therefore, when you observe life closely, many a time, you will find individuals with predominantly masculine traits born as women and those with feminine traits being assigned the role of a man. It is the way of the universe to balance the tendencies of our soul personality. The universe does this as it understands the fact that as souls, we need to have the right balance of both masculine and feminine traits. Or more specifically, the right set of tendencies that combine into a wholesome personality. So, through this process, the universe helps souls correct any imbalances and attain the right mix of both feminine and masculine traits as both are essential to have a balanced soul personality.

This is important because by balancing our soul personality, we also balance out the set of karmas that we perform or clear out in a given lifetime and even the subsequent ones for that matter. This is because the tendencies of a soul influence the karma it performs, which, in turn, influences the soul's destiny. Hence, we can say that the personality of a soul (which is its combined set of tendencies) has a direct impact on its life and the circumstances it encounters. It also has a direct influence on energy exchanges that the soul has with other human beings and during various situations and events throughout the entire period of its birth. Therefore, the tendencies of a soul have a direct correlation with its intentions, thoughts, words, and actions, which together combine to make its karma and destiny.

Another reason why a balanced soul personality is crucial for every soul is that it helps the soul with its evolution and growth and also enhances its power. If the soul personality is flawed or imbalanced in any way, it has an adverse influence on the soul's decision-making capability and also incites negative thoughts. Not only that, but the negative impact of all this has a direct bearing on the soul's karmas, leading to troubled lifetimes and difficult destinies.

So, we can see how important it is to have a balanced soul personality! It is the very basis of one's given life path and what one is likely to create as their future and destiny. This also explains why we must not draw conclusions on the basis of our physical forms because a soul cannot be limited to any label and more specifically, to any gender. What really matters is that regardless of our physical form, we should live correctly and do what is right.

But whether we do realise the same as important or not, the universe always has its way to set us right. For instance, a soul born as a male could have a larger set of feminine traits in its personality and can be quite nurturing, providing, caring, sensitive, and emotional. But for it to survive the cut-throat world of business and work life, which is going to be a very likely part of its journey, this soul will need to balance its feminine traits with its masculine side. It will need to learn to be a little unabashed, bold, courageous, mentally strong, emotionally stable, and pragmatic in order to do what is needed in the given role. And even though this may be way out of its comfort zone, given the soul's real personality or tendencies, it will be pushed to adapt to its new role by embracing those qualities, which the universe has chosen to make a part of its personality through the assigned role. And if the soul resists this balancing act, it is highly unlikely that it will succeed in the given role and will have to go through another lifetime or perhaps several lifetimes with a similar role in order to achieve the necessary balance.

Similarly, a soul having acquired a female form can exhibit a more pronounced male temperament. That is, it can have qualities such as being headstrong, dogmatic, overly practical, aggressive, etc., that may not complement the assigned role. But the fact that a specific role is a mandate for this soul, it will have to develop its sensitive, nurturing, flexible, gentle, and loving side. This would require the soul to balance out its rather dominant masculine traits with certain feminine qualities.

Another point that needs a mention here is the fact that to succeed in any given role in any lifetime, a soul needs both masculine and feminine qualities. Because, as said earlier, the soul by itself is not gender specific and life always operates out of situations that demand one to think as a man as well as a woman! A one-dimensional approach never quite works when it comes to successfully handling life. Therefore, every soul needs to put both masculine and feminine traits into practice in order to crack the code of good karma and boost its own powers.

So, each lifetime provides a fair opportunity to a soul to cultivate qualities and tendencies in order to balance out its personality and help it evolve. No matter how challenging this may seem, moving out of its comfort zone is the only way to achieve this.

Thus, we can see that the universe does have its way of balancing things in each one of us and this is precisely why we come into this world!

Chapter 5

THE UNIVERSE RESPONDS TO OUR ENERGY

As discussed before, we, as souls, accumulate many layers of tendencies through our innumerable births. All these patterns of habit, patterns of thought processes, patterns of feelings, intentions, emotions, and actions lend a certain character to each one of us. So, we are who we are, not because of our present birth. Rather we are who we are because as souls we have operated through a specific psyche for a very long time. In other words, it is over a period of many births, many interactions, many energy exchanges, and many karmas performed that we get entrenched in a certain personality. And it is this long-standing personality, this hidden but powerful energy, to which the universe responds.

As mentioned above, the universe comes back to us, not with what we want but with who we are or how we are. An important point to note here is that the universe has no agendas or plans of its own. It does not think of punishing or rewarding us. It does not want good or bad for us. For the universe is absolutely neutral or impartial in that sense. It only reflects our own energy to us, our own subconscious recording.

Therefore, we can think positively and do positive things, but if our inner personality or the subtle energy, also known as soul, is deficient in positivity, or positive tendencies to be more specific, then we may not get the desired result. This is because the universe is not aligned with our rational mind or our brainpower. Instead, the universe is in sync with our soul and therefore, we attract the sort of experiences more in sync with our soul personality than our thoughts. Yes, our energy or our soul personality acts like a magnet!

So, say if our energy within is white, the universe will respond with similar energy or event, situation, outcome, etc. If our energy is blue, then something similar will come back, even though we might be thinking of a different colour. And then there can be times when we are thinking black but since our soul quality may be white, the universe can really surprise us by sending along something pure and beautiful. In such a scenario, we must understand that despite the black in our thoughts and feelings or even the environment that we live in, the universe remains cognizant of the true colour of our energy or our soul personality.

This somewhere explains why in this world, we can find people, who after doing wrong things, get away easily and not be punished. This also explains why some people, who choose to act right, can be found suffering. For what they receive has little to do with how they think, act, or feel in the present time. Instead, it has more to do with their soul personality made up of qualities/tendencies that they have accumulated over several lifetimes. Though needless to say, one still needs to think, feel, and act right at all times in order to keep things favourable and positive and also to turn things around. Because even though it takes some time for the universe to get aligned with one's present state of being, the darker tones of one's energy eventually do transform by constantly mixing it with the positive tones and vice versa. Let us understand the same with an example.

Say, we have a palette full of dark hues and we want to turn them a few shades lighter. So, what do we do? We simply keep mixing white into them or some other lighter colour, until what is dark transforms into a lighter hue. Though of course, this may take some time, patience, and effort, we will eventually achieve the desired result. Such is the case with the colour of our soul or our energy. It takes some time, patience, and constant effort to transform this energy into a more positive and higher force.

What is important to understand here is the fact that there are all kinds of right and wrong tendencies recorded in a soul. These recorded tendencies combine into a full-blown personality. And it is this soul personality that acts as a magnet and attracts results that match its energy. This is the reason why you may find certain unintelligent or incapable people achieve great success at times. This is also the reason why you may find the most capable and deserving individuals struggle to get the success that they are deserving of. It is all linked to their energy or the soul personality they have cultivated over lifetimes!

Therefore, for each one of us, the thing that is absolutely imperative in this given lifetime is to understand life beyond what is tangible. Meaning, that we need to dedicate time to the self in order to understand the subtler but more powerful aspects of our being. Because unless we make the effort to understand our deeper personality and explore our inner patterns, we are likely to remain clueless about why life happens the way it does. This is imperative, especially for those, who may be tired of trying to change things for the better and haven't yet received a positive response from the universe. And as for people who are happy and satisfied with what they have, it is again important to tune into their deeper personality, to explore, understand, and be aware of their energy, their soul personality. The fact that they are here shows that there is scope for growth and that they need to make the most of this opportunity.

Chapter 6
REST IN PEACE

Perhaps the most widely used phrase for anyone who leaves this world is: Rest In Peace. Despite its extensive use, I wonder how many of us actually understand what it truly means. Of course, through this phrase, we are wishing well for the departed soul. But there is a deeper implication behind the usage of this phrase. We feel that when a person encounters death, then rest and peace are the two things they are sure to attain as this world is so challenging, demanding, and stressful. And therefore, we somewhere genuinely want to believe that rest and peace are delivered to us in death.

Another reason for us to believe in this notion is that we do not know what lies beyond this world of matter. So, we like to believe that once we are out of our mortal form, we will be free and can rest in the soul world and be at peace.

There is yet another reason for this belief. Many of us look at death in a rather negative light and consider it as the darkest and the most traumatic experience for a soul. So, we wish peace and rest for a departed soul, which may help it heal faster, post this turbulent encounter.

The truth is that all these are just conjectures, which prompt us to use this highly verbalised thought today. But regardless of why we use these words, one thing that comes across quite evidently is the fact that we neither understand life nor do we understand death. Most times, we say things just for the sake of saying or as a gesture of respect and well-wishing, but the true relevance of peace and rest in the context of death, as well as life, is something we are oblivious to.

Now, let us explore the relevance of this popular term a bit further and understand how a soul can actually rest in peace once it leaves this world of forms.

Before we answer these questions, it is important to recapitulate the fact that what the soul carries along with it, once it leaves the body, is its set of tendencies that combine together to form its true personality or the state of its energy. But this soul personality or energy may have been an unconscious factor in the life of a soul when it existed inside the physical form. Because while a person is alive, it is the conscious mind that remains in control of its choices, responses, and decisions and acts as the primary guiding force through the soul's mortal journey.

However, everything that the soul experiences in its various lifetimes, or what it exchanges in the form of energy or karma, gets recorded in the soul's personality. And while in the physical form, these recordings are often conveyed to it by the voice of its subconscious. But because we rarely access this voice during the course of our life and are habitually guided by the conscious mind, we seldom get to know the real self. So, after death, when we get detached from the conscious mind, all that is left with is our set of tendencies acquired during the course of our life. And these tendencies and impressions which are also a soul's recordings, translate into the actual state of the soul. For example, if a soul largely remained peaceful, happy, and contented regardless of what it encountered during the course of its life then this implies that these are the tendencies that it has cultivated or gathered and the same will be the state of the soul once it is detached from the body. In other words, this means that the soul will rest in peace. Similarly, if a soul remained stressed, hurt, and anxious regardless of what it encountered during its human journey, then for such a soul to be in peace and rest after death is going to be challenging.

From this, we can see the significance and impact of tendencies on a soul's human journey and even in its afterlife. But this is not to say that what a soul encounters during the course of its human journey or its experiences do not matter. The fact is that experiences too play a crucial role as they have a direct bearing on how a soul feels, thinks, behaves, and acts. But how a soul handles these experiences and how much power it gains or loses in the process determines whether or not it is able to rest in peace.

This underscores the importance of human beings staying in harmony with life, acquiring the necessary wisdom, and operating through self-awareness or staying spiritually aligned. These things ensure that the influence of external aspects on the inner mechanism remains largely positive and in healthy control. We can find people in this world who have the capacity to endure a lot of difficulties, hardships, and trauma with ease. It all depends on one's attitude towards life and one's capacity to handle it, which directly connect to the tendencies the soul has brought into its present life that help in encountering experiences with dignity and poise. This also decides the kind of tendencies a soul accumulates during the span of a lifetime. Also, if a soul is reborn, it will continue being in the state that it was in during its previous birth or in its final years in the previous form. This explains why some infants who are born in the most chaotic households and to parents who may have the most challenging personalities can have a rather peaceful and happy demeanour. The opposite can be true as well.

Infants and children belonging to a very peaceful, calm, and serene environment, where people are largely happy and contented, can have a personality of utter unrest.

In all such cases, what comes across strongly is the personality or the tendencies of the soul. These tendencies are more pronounced and active in a child, especially, before the child develops a conscious mind and begins to speak and discern things through a different lens.

Thus, we can see the importance of our soul personality and why should we pay attention to what we accumulate in thoughts, emotions, and feelings for as long as we live! Also, this means that for a soul to rest in peace, it should have lived and experienced a life of peace. It is like any travel for that matter. If the journey has been rough and bumpy due to which we become cranky and miserable, we are likely to feel exhaustion, anger, and unrest once we reach our destination and even long after, when we reflect on the experience. The recording has already happened during the course of the journey and all we do is relive the emotion. This is exactly what happens to a soul during this human journey. If it chooses to remain unperturbed and peaceful while on the journey, then rest and peace will be the soul's natural state post death.

However, remaining calm and at ease can get challenging at certain times. And then, it is not necessary that a soul's experiences and relationships or even the environment that it lives in will allow it to remain calm and peaceful in life. One can be dragged into chaos and confusion and slip into depression and anxiety without even realising it.

So, to be able to live in peace and subsequently, rest in peace, one needs to attach greater value to the way one encounters life. The external factors may not always be in one's control, as they largely depend on the karma or karmic debts of the soul. But one thing that is in a soul's control is the kind of response it gives to these external factors which can save it from accumulating or strengthening negative tendencies.

Here are a few things that can help a soul provide the right response to life:

1. Understanding one's higher self through the lens of higher wisdom
2. Self-reflection
3. Self-observation
4. Self-awareness, particularly the awareness of how one feels while facing various situations and also how one responds
5. Feeding the right information to the mind
6. Improving the quality of one's thoughts
7. Building inner resources through positive reinforcement
8. Not focusing on trying to change the negative aspects but consciously choosing and using positive traits
9. Working on one's emotional maturity
10. Inner evolution and transformation
11. Inner work to reach one's higher self

These are some of the ways through which we can move out of our ignorance, which is the cause of all trouble. These aspects can help us live more consciously, dissolve negative tendencies, and bring more peace and power into one's being.

Chapter 7
MANAGING INNER AND OUTER WORLDS

In life, we have the responsibility of managing two worlds. The first is our outer world, comprising relationships, work, activities, education, transactions, travel, society, culture, physical environment, etc. And the second is our inner world, which is all about our thoughts, feelings, emotions, intentions, personality, and behaviour. And while the majority of us believe that we are here to participate in the outer world and honour its various requirements, what we fail to realise is that there is also an inner world, which requires equal time and attention.

Overall, both these worlds are equally important and relevant and both have a significant impact on our journey as a soul, but while a soul is in a human body, it is the inner world which actually takes centre stage. This is because everything that happens around a soul in the outer world is simply to draw the necessary attention towards what lies within! Therefore, the outer world is more of a trigger for a soul to draw its attention to an entirely different and subtler world within. In order words, the real purpose of every relationship, every event, every transaction, every situation, and every action that we encounter in the outer world is to actually help us realise and explore the inner world that lies within all of us. And life through its various situations keeps directing us to understand what lies within us. It creates drama, makes us go through certain experiences, and puts us in specific environments that bring the opportunity to become self-aware and understand what lies within as tendencies or as the subtler self. Let's understand this better with the help of an example.

There is a minor accident and the cars of both the parties involved (person A and person B) get dented. Person A responds to the situation with aggression, while person B, though being in the same situation, does not react so sharply. Person A hurls abuses and wants complete compensation while person B wants to work out a suitable course of action for both parties.

The example shows how different people respond differently to the same crisis. In the above example, the accident, which is a part of the drama of life, a part of our outer world, was the trigger that elicited two different responses or tendencies, which, in turn, reflect two different kinds of energies.

Hence, we can conclude that we all have different tendencies and life tries to make us aware of them by putting us through myriad experiences in the outer world. So, if we think that whatever happens in our outer world is just an event or a situation or a chance occurrence, then we completely miss out on the bigger purpose of these events. And that is the reason we rarely learn our lessons and we rarely progress as souls.

Life can also help bring greater self-awareness through contrasting inner and outer worlds. Take the case of some people living the life of a renunciate in dedicated spiritual environments. People who teach the art of selfless living in public (their outer world) and deliver sermons on how to live an egoless life and build inner peace and calm. But these very people, at times, can be seen acting quite contrary to their teachings and philosophies. In other words, their inner world responses are different from their outer reality. And this is the reason why their pious and plain outer world can seem in stark contrast to their deep-rooted egoic tendencies of arrogance, attachments, and at times even greed. So, in such cases, the purpose of life is to make these people aware of their inner impurities through an outer environment that is completely opposite to their inner self.

The complete opposite of this situation can be true as well, i.e., there are people who are living in a highly materialistic environment and yet, their inner personality is simplistic and egoless. These are the sort of people who operate more out of humility, contentment, peace, and a grounded approach and respond to the outer world through detachment from labels, names, recognition, and materiality. And so, even though they may not be living the life of a sage, their tendencies can be of a sage.

This goes to show that at times, you can put someone in a spiritual sanctuary and yet, they may pursue rank and status there, and you can put someone in a marketplace, and they may pursue their goals and gains with absolute selflessness or with the aim to do more philanthropy. This also proves that the soul personality of any individual or his or her inner world is what makes one think, act, and behave in a certain way regardless of how their outer world is.

Hence, we can conclude that the outer world never quite dictates or determines how we behave, act, or respond to a stimulus or to an environment and rather, it is always the choice or the influence of our inner world or soul personality.

Here, what is important to understand is that our outer world job or situation should be considered as a means to the end. And with the end being nothing more than greater self-awareness, everything happening in the outer world for us is simply a means to generate the same. This awareness is the very foundation of our evolution as a soul! It tells us about the level of peace, power, emotional balance, happiness, love, humility, and compassion we have within. It also tells us about how much anger, resentment, anxiety, jealousy, ego, greed, lust, and attachments we harbour. And each time a stimulus from the outer world triggers any of these qualities that are present in us, we are introduced to our deepest self or our real personality that has resulted from deep impressions and an accumulation of various tendencies, through various lifetimes. Hence, the significance of awareness can never be overstated if we want to work on the self or better the self.

Our soul personality is indeed who we are, because mostly, when we perceive something in the outer world, we do not consciously choose to behave in a certain way. The response is largely instinctive or spontaneous! So, there are times when we choose forgiveness over punishment, even when the situation demands that we punish the guilty. And we act in this way because there is compassion and maturity in the soul personality as it has more peace within than anger.

Hence, our inner world largely dictates or determines how we behave, act, or respond to a stimulus or to an environment. This explains why different people respond to the same situation differently and why people act contrary to their physical environments.

A sage in a human costume can have the tendencies of an entrepreneur while a businessman can be a sage within.

But what is important to understand in the given context is that a person, who might have been a thorough businessman in a past life can be born as a sage in this life so that he or she cultivates a soul personality, which is essentially non-material or spiritual. And similarly, a sage can be born as a businessman, so that he or she learns to be street smart, pragmatic, tactful, ambitious, clever, worldly-wise, and hardworking. This happens so that they both eliminate the anomalies of their deeper personality and balance out their material side with the spiritual, so that there are no extremes. And that is the very reason their outer world is a stark contrast to their inner mechanism, which helps them cultivate that side of their personality, which is essentially deficient.

Then, our outer world is where we can offset our karmic balances through energy exchanges, transactions, and interactions that we must engage in, as there are dues with other souls or with situations that we need to settle or clear. Dues that are carried forward from previous lives and which make each new life an opportunity to pay back. And settling karma or giving back to other souls or even receiving for that matter makes this event of life very significant for each one of us. For it offers us a rare opportunity to clear debts and receive benefits, which not only make us lighter but also help other souls achieve their purpose in life.

This doesn't mean that we just focus on what we give and receive as life is not just about human transactions or our involvement with other people. These are just a part of life and not all of it, which many of us wrongly consider as the only thing. As a result, we seek endless gratification in the outer world, through people, through our work, and through objects, pleasures, activities, and the physical attributes of this world. And sometimes, due to this endless pursuit, an entire lifetime goes by without us realising the existence of the all-important world within.

Thus, we need to remember that this precious human birth is not given to us just to experience pleasure or pain, or to eat, drink, work, enjoy, travel, celebrate, and be merry, or to take certain education and a certain profession, or to earn labels and tags, which sadly in this body-conscious, material world defines who we are. It is also not given in order to be with our family or people who are dear to us or to dedicate our life to a mission or to help the world and its people. Each of these aforementioned factors are a mere catalyst to our story and not the story itself.

The fact is that this invaluable human birth has been given to us to simply become self-aware, raise our consciousness through greater self-awareness, eliminate the darkness from our soul, and increase soul power with an accumulation of the right tendencies. In other words, human birth is given to us so that we can deal with ourselves better, simply by reflecting on the self, understanding the self, and improving the self.

Each birth is the greatest event in our journey as a soul. And only those who understand this are able to manage their inner and outer worlds well and fulfil their purpose in life.

Chapter 8
OUR HUMAN ROLES

One of the most stunning truths in life is that though there are billions of people on this planet, there is just one born for a role assigned individually to each of us in a given lifetime. Each one of us has been assigned an exclusive and well-defined purpose. So, all we need to do is live and explore our individual roles to the fullest and most importantly, keep in mind, for what purpose and why this specific role has come our way. Because once we realise our true purpose in life, there is every chance that we will play our individual parts well. However, should we choose to live without knowing why and for what reason we are here, then it will not just be a waste of our potential, but this will also create aimless living. Also, not knowing one's assigned role and the reason for it often leads to a lot of illusions, misconceptions, doubts, and even disenchantment at times. We will explore this further in the following topics.

Significance and Purpose of Human Roles

As we have already established, we are all souls playing a human role. The roles given to us are on the basis of our travel time on earth which is determined by the number of previous lifetimes and roles in the physical form. It is also determined by the specific set of karmas *(prarabhdha)* that we need to burn or dissolve from our total karmic balance sheet *(sanchita karmas)* as carried forward in each lifetime. But more importantly, our role and our allotted time depend on our level of evolution and state of maturity as denoted by our tendencies. We need more time when our tendencies are complex and need sustained awareness and effort to transform.

Each of our roles is distinct because as souls, we come from different backgrounds, different journeys, and with different life patterns that have been travelling with us through our different lifetimes. And since each of us travels at a different pace and has been on this material plane for a different number of lifetimes, this is the reason why our lives cannot be defined by mere external factors or by our place and position in this world. Instead, it is largely defined by our soul quality or soul power, which of course, varies from soul to soul.

So, the souls that have lived a higher number of human births would think, act, and feel differently and will be given a role that is a bit more demanding than the rest. Demanding here would mean spiritually demanding, not karmically because having lived a significant number of lifetimes, these souls have settled their share of karmic debts. However, since settling karma is challenging in several ways, these souls would now be drained and exhausted. So, such souls would now require adequate rest and rejuvenation and would need to become more mindful of rebuilding their spiritual resources, their inner powers. It becomes important for such souls to work on their spiritual side and focus less on the material or at least, have a healthy balance of the material and spiritual. Also, after being in the cycle of rebirth for much longer, one's mind becomes deeply conditioned in a certain way, something these souls would need to work on and alter by changing their outlook towards life and understanding their deeper self.

Therefore, inner awakening becomes imperative for these souls not only for their evolution but also for the rejuvenation of their bored and tired minds. And this boredom is bound to occur after one repeatedly goes through the same material grind, over the course of many lives which, in turn, makes these souls drift away from the dynamics of regular day-to-day existence in their ongoing journey. These souls reject the material chase at the subconscious level and seek something that can energise them and empower them. This includes things that are more inward driven and help with preserving energy as well as invoke more positive tendencies and help realign them with their powerful self.

So, in order to alter conditioning and reprogram their own mind or thought process and reset tendencies, such souls tend to gravitate towards spiritual studies. But it may not always be a spiritual path. It can even be a life of simplicity and anonymity or a life of quiet creative pursuits or just plain devotion to something that contributes to their inner well-being, like serving nature in some way or doing things that help and heal humanity. Through such activities, these souls are able to restore their lost powers.

And so, souls which have led this earthly life for a longer period need to divert attention towards activities that can help give rest to their conscious mind and make them more intuitive. In other words, they need their mind and intellect to return to their roots, which essentially means creative and spiritual aspects. And once this happens, these souls can alter their conditioning from several lifetimes and live with greater awareness of who they truly are, which quite naturally promotes peace, strength, love, humility, and happiness in them.

So, we can see how we acquire roles that are necessary for our growth. Here, one needs to take an important fact into consideration that any role, by no means is given to any of us to teach something to others. Rather, it is given to us to help us learn what we have come here to learn.

Different Roles for Different Souls

As mentioned above, souls who have travelled for a longer period and have taken more rebirths in this world of forms are old souls. And during the course of their lifetime, it is precisely these souls who are likely to feel out of place in a material environment or who are not able to find material success despite their best efforts because their given role now demands that they pursue something else. Something that is more elevated, transformative, and the opposite of what they have been doing in their prior experiences. So, most old souls need to opt out of the rat race and start on a journey of self-exploration and healing.

But should they still keep pushing the self to achieve material or worldly success, then most likely, they'll continue to suffer and will need to come back to a similar role in another life in order to evolve.

Then there are roles which are more suited for the competitive, cut-throat material world. And here, one finds souls which have less exposure to the world of forms. Having encountered or experienced a lesser number of past births, these souls are far more energised, less challenged, and can be more ambitious when compared to old souls. Their experiences or interactions—aspects which alter soul conditioning and keep expanding a soul's karmic memory, thereby taking away its peace—may be far lesser in comparison.

So, they need to go through all kinds of experiences, which then gradually alter their soul personality. These experiences revolve around everything material, primarily because, as souls on a journey, when we come on the material plane, we first need to encounter everything about this plane, as only when we are truly experienced and perhaps even exhausted or saturated, will we look for something deeper and more meaningful or something entirely different. But not until we are fully exhausted, not until we have had all kinds of experiences and transactions with other souls and lived the drama to the fullest. After all, does this not happen otherwise also? Say, we travel to a new place and when we reach, we want to explore every aspect, every nook and corner of the place.

Then gradually, after we have travelled around the place over and over again, after we have repeatedly enjoyed the beauty and surroundings of the place, after we have formed associations and contacts, and after we have made a home and built a settlement, a community, and social network, there comes a point when boredom begins to set in, and we crave for something new. The familiarity of the place, the monotony, and the lack of newness and excitement begins to tire us a bit and it is only then that we begin to look for change. This is precisely the journey we all undertake as souls!

And until we become satiated in the material world, until we feel a lack of excitement in the worldly entrapments, and until we feel the need to seek something beyond this world, we remain happy doing the run-of-the-mill stuff. We feel happy chasing a career, being in love, being married, raising children, paying the bills, indulging in material pleasures and comforts and pursuing everything that excites the senses.

And that's the beauty of life. It gives room to all kinds of souls to mature and evolve at different speeds. But then, at no point can we escape what we need, which again varies.

And it is through our assigned role that we must try and understand what that exactly is. This is the only way we can find peace in our lives.

Importance of Playing Different Roles

As human beings, only by playing different roles across one or many lifetimes can we understand our full potential. For our consciousness expands through our experience of human life, the experience of our roles and so, we need to essay different roles.

Take the case of actors in theatre and films. Every actor remains keen to play different roles in order to explore his or her full potential. Every new and demanding role allows them to develop their acting skills and explore untouched dimensions. It also allows them to challenge themselves, which again is essential for an actor to evolve in his or her professional journey. This is the reason why no actor wants to get stuck with repetitive parts or get typecast. Also, experimenting with different roles keeps an actor's enthusiasm alive. On the other hand, if an actor is repeatedly cast in similar roles, they begin to feel less excited which can lead to a loss of interest in acting. Succinctly put, lack of satisfaction and challenge depletes inspiration which, in turn, eventually depletes peace within the actor.

This is exactly the case with souls, for we are here to play different roles in this world and as we transition across lifetimes, we enrich our experience as well as the understanding of the self or our soul personality. And we need these varied experiences to explore our full potential and to evolve and progress to a higher state.

Though sometimes, we have to repeat certain roles in different lifetimes. This happens when we have not played the role well, not learnt what we were meant to, or not adapted fully to the role in a single lifetime. So, if we are unable to adopt the true virtues of a given role in the time when we are in that role, then that role will come back to us in another lifetime and perhaps, it may keep coming back, till we achieve the true purpose of that role. But what is certain is that all of us play all possible roles over many-many births. And the technique of past life regression has repeatedly proven the same! So, we can play the primary role of a mother in one life, and then a father in the next, a wife in one and a husband in another, a son in one, a daughter in another, or we can take on a different profession or inhabit a different culture and geography. And like this, till we have explored all roles and perfected them, explored our full potential as a soul and, nurtured qualities that are exclusive to each role, we will find it hard to feel that sense of disenchantment.

Disenchantment is essentially a spiritual or mystical intervention which is vital for seeking a deeper aspect beyond these worldly roles and for refuelling our lost powers. And this is something that a soul receives only after playing varied roles through its innumerable journeys spread across different lifetimes.

Significance of Valuing a Given Role

An important point to realise here is that we are all born unique and each of our roles is as special as any other role. Also, no two roles can be similar, as we have been travelling and evolving at different speeds. In terms of living in the world of forms, some of us may be older and more experienced, some in between and some might still be new, fresh, and raring to go. And so, depending on the age of our soul, a particular role is given to us. Since we are travelling at different speeds and different time lengths, it also means that we all have different lessons to learn, different things to experience, and different realisations to go through. Therefore, no two roles or even destinies can be similar.

This means that the next time you think, 'I wish my life was like so and so', think again! Perhaps, you have already lived that part which you admire right now. Perhaps, that role is not the thing that can help you evolve in your journey. Perhaps, it is one role you have already mastered and so, it attracts you, simply because it reminds you of your comfort zone. But then, our comfort zone delays our inner progress and growth. Therefore, a different role than what makes one comfortable is necessary. A role where one is likely to flourish the most and be challenged and compelled to use their hidden powers, which would otherwise remain dormant if they were in a role that did not demand their use. Therefore, regardless of the nature of the role that one has been assigned, one must pay attention to and value their acquired role.

So, we should consider every role as a blessing as it can be one's ticket to greater and better lifetimes with higher possibilities for our evolutionary journey. But this can only happen if we know and understand what our role demands internally from us and play it to perfection. We also need to understand that should we not choose to play our role well, should we ignore what it demands and aspire for something different, we would not just be wasting precious time but writing a destiny of repetition, along with intense hard work and increasing boredom. This is because if we ignore what our role demands from us or if we lust for something that has been given to someone else, we will be born again and again with the same role. And this repetition only gets more challenging with every birth. So, we need to understand what our present role intends to teach us or cultivate in us as tendencies.

Can you imagine, coming back to playing the same role over and over again? Even in our regular lives, is it not difficult for us to do the same things again and again? Does it not tire us or bewilder us? Does it not make us want to kill the monotony and move to something new? Similarly, think about playing a human role over and over again over various lifetimes. Even though subconsciously, we may feel exhausted and uninspired, we are left with no option but to keep playing the same role till it has served its higher purpose. And if we go on living ignorantly and unconsciously, oblivious to our role's real significance and the value it can add to our state of being, we will continue to go in circles.

Therefore, instead of questioning our circumstantial reality and not wanting to live the life that we are meant to, all we need to do is live in the moment, be attentive to our role, and pay heed to what it expects out of us.

Chapter 9
RECOGNISING OLD SOULS

The human population of the planet has exploded since the industrial revolution.

The population was 1 billion at the start of the 19th century which has now grown to nearly 8 billion 20 years into the 21st century. The figures also reveal that more and more souls have inhabited this world of forms over a span of the last 220 years.

We needn't go too much into the statistics of it nor should we draw imaginary assumptions about where souls reside before they come here to play their part over different lifetimes. Some secrets are best left to the universe and humans need not know everything. But given the population statistics, what we need to understand is that there are some souls (a far lesser number) that have taken several rebirths and are travelling the cycle of birth and death for a much longer time and continue to do so, even now.

These souls are old souls as they have spent a long time in the world of forms. Even though it may not be so easy to identify these souls or to even know if one is an old soul, one can still understand something about them just by making an effort to explore their soul psyche or personality which they have acquired over time in the world of forms. We can do so by placing them under the scanner of preferences, attributes, reality, and quest and analysing the results to understand how old souls would be operating. We know for a fact that, given their wider exposure to human life and countless experiences, old souls would clearly enjoy the most distinct preferences, which may not be so common among the larger section of the population. In fact, they can be quite the opposite in their choices as well as in their responses to people and life in general. They can also have the most unique set of characteristics and habits that belong only to them! Also, when it comes to their quest in life, old souls may have the most unusual and uncommon aspirations, goals, desires, and pursuits, primarily due to their much longer journey on this material plane.

So, here is how one can best recognise old souls. Given below is a list with four relevant categories identifying the primary characteristics and inclinations of old souls. Needless to mention that not all of these patterns will be a hundred per cent present in every old soul. But by and large, all old souls can be collectively identified or distinguished from the vast majority through the following patterns belonging to four broad categories.

Their Preferences

1. Mind over matter
2. Inner abundance
3. Inner balance
4. Non-material activities (a balance of material and spiritual pursuits)
5. Giving a more evolved meaning to what's ancient (culture, faith, belief systems, etc.)
6. Minimalism
7. Escaping city life
8. Non-crowded places

9. Small, intimate settings
10. Meaningful social interactions
11. Enlightening conversations
12. Making the most of what is
13. Greener environments
14. To be free of worldly desires
15. Self-exploration/self-discovery
16. Solitude or me-time
17. Self-awareness
18. Simplified existence
19. Silence
20. Knowledge of philosophy, mysticism, and spirituality
21. Self-improvement
22. Self-empowerment and healing
23. Living in the present moment
24. Doing more, talking less
25. Rationalising religious texts
26. Logic over emotions and impulse
27. Creative pursuits such as poetry, art, music, etc.
28. Simple joys of living
29. Meditative practices over ritualistic or traditional ones
30. Sharing wisdom
31. Giving equal attention to mind, body, and spirit
32. Exploring new and liberating beliefs
33. Challenging and changing redundant practices
34. Egoless living, which includes distancing the self from the ego-inflating ways of the world
35. Giving and not hoarding

Their Attributes

1. Sensitive
2. Nonconformist
3. Deeper intelligence
4. Curious mind
5. Uninspired by what's worldly
6. Detached
7. Intuitive
8. Self-sustained
9. Low profile
10. Thinkers, not dreamers
11. Curious about other dimensions
12. Explorers of ancient history and science
13. Disinterested in popular means of entertainment
14. Drawn to observation, research, and study
15. Consider nature as a good company
16. Not too fond of shopping, clubbing, partying, etc.
17. Realist
18. Unconventional and unorthodox
19. Relate to God as formless
20. Believe that God is one
21. Enjoy humble tasks/chores
22. Empathetic
23. Unpretentious
24. Straightforward
25. Good listeners
26. Love privacy
27. See the beauty in darkness

28. Accept death with maturity
29. Believe in rebirth
30. Understand karma
31. Reject superstitions or fear-based beliefs
32. Feel they have a higher purpose
33. Enjoy a non-transactional relationship with God
34. Believe in oneness

Their Reality

1. Have little to no material cravings
2. Speak less and understand more
3. Understand other people and the self beyond the limiting references of labels
4. Can give up worldly temptations and desires
5. Happy and satisfied with a few material possessions
6. Constantly work to build inner peace and maturity
7. Spiritually aligned but not bound to any specific path
8. They accept what is
9. Can meditate
10. Can access inner stillness
11. Invest in reaching a higher consciousness
12. Have unique and powerful thoughts
13. Have the least expectations
14. Free from the social, cultural, and religious dogmas
15. Accept suffering as necessary for one's growth
16. Understand the ego as the enemy
17. Prioritise working on the ego
18. Lead quieter lives
19. Remain unaffected by what others think of them

20. Do more charity or non-profit work
21. Don't easily give in to fear
22. At times, they can be lost and clueless
23. At times, they can be disenchanted with the world
24. Cannot fit into the rat race
25. Focus on goodness more than success
26. Cannot lead a conventional life

Their Quest

1. Unlearning the old and experimenting with something ncw
2. Mental and emotional rejuvenation and growth
3. Inner well-being
4. Redefining the self
5. Understanding and aligning with one's spiritual truth
6. Understanding time, life, and destiny
7. Understanding divinity which is different from understanding God
8. Restoring the powers and virtues of one's higher self
9. Emotional independence
10. Decoding the intangible, the metaphysical
11. Seeking answers to life and death
12. Creating a new and evolved philosophy of life
13. Dissolving old conditioning
14. A sense of newness
15. Experience of something deeper and mature
16. Having zero emotional baggage
17. Conscious living

18. Self -transformation
19. Freedom from the world of forms
20. Enlightenment

The significance of understanding old souls arises from the fact that not everyone on this material plane would be inclined towards exploring and understanding the deeper meaning of life, inner transformation, spirituality, and higher wisdom. Such a life is mostly undertaken by those few who have reached a point in their human journey, where they feel satiated by material things and have become unattached to this world of forms. Also, such souls have minimal karmic bondage as they have completed their karmic payback over the course of several lifetimes.

As mentioned earlier, old souls are definitely a minority because the majority of souls seek and wish to experience this world of forms as they have unfulfilled desires and therefore, the urge to indulge in worldly pleasures, human interactions, and activities. And these are things they should experience because it is only through wide-ranging experiences and exposure to different human roles that they can achieve evolution and growth. The complete experience of human life is also necessary for souls who haven't completed their set of karmic paybacks and until they do that, they won't get the opportunity for the necessary learning, which is integral to change. After all, our karmic balances act as a distraction and hurdle to our spiritual awakening and growth. They take away a lot of our time and attention and keep us constantly involved in settling our debts with other souls on this journey. Therefore, all souls must evolve organically and not by some sort of external force. For evolution cannot happen through pressure. It only happens through inner will and awakening.

Chapter 10

WE ACQUIRE ROLES THAT HELP US IMPROVE

As souls, when we are transiting from one birth to another, we acquire a specific role on the basis of our karmic balances as well as our accumulated tendencies or what can be termed as our soul personality. This is a role that we need to play in our new life. A role that is demanding in its own unique way, as its primary aim is to enable us to work on those aspects of our soul personality that perhaps we are weakest at. So, it could be any role, but its primary objective is to drive us towards cleansing, improving, and empowering our soul personality during that particular lifetime.

Of course, how much effort we put into a specific role, how much we learn from it, or how much we transform while playing that role is a matter of free will. But one thing is certain that the role we acquire is meant to work towards elevating our soul personality. Thus, we need to have greater self-awareness along with a deeper understanding of what our role demands from us and what we can do in it in order to become a better being.

We need to assess how our given role holds many precious secrets to our soul personality. And if we pay attention to it and involve ourselves a little more deeply with our role and also with the life around us and reflect on what it is trying to teach us, we can become enlightened.

We shall exactly know what is it that we have come to build within our psychological and spiritual state. We will also get an idea about what is deficient in our soul personality and what is the best way to bring the necessary balance.

Also, somewhere at the subconscious level, we all remain aware of why we are playing a certain part in our life. Our role keeps nudging our mind in different ways and keeps pushing us to inculcate certain qualities that transform or elevate us as a person. Yet, it is only an attentive being that finds it easier to tackle the assigned role and do full justice to it. And it does so by tapping into the subconscious and by making the effort to understand things by examining their own thoughts and feelings from time to time. On the other hand, if we are internally not well aligned with our role or when our tendencies lack the strength and maturity to handle the role, it is highly likely that we will falter and make mistakes. But it is precisely in such moments that we need to assess the self instead of judging the role. In fact, it is during moments of failure, conflicts, and difficulty that we can get the most valuable insights. And we can handle anything in life with the help of these insights.

Take the case of a sportsman. If he or she isn't performing well, they don't blame the stadium, the field, the turf, or the team. Instead, they work on themselves and improve their own game, their own strengths, and performance. And that's how they win. Similarly, we need to do what makes us better at playing our role to perfection. And for that, we need to look within.

But the problem is that most of us aren't able to do so. And in such a scenario, all we need to remember is that we are playing a role which we haven't played before and hence, we can't be good at it. It's a territory with which we aren't familiar. And so, we need to first assess the self in the context of the role and find out what more can we incorporate in our own personality to make this role a success. Once we are able to do this, it will be a whole lot easier to dissolve all major weaknesses and incorporate those tendencies that the role aims to help embed in our personality.

The reason why we are born in a specific environment, a specific family or societal setting, a specific set of circumstances, etc., is because they together channel our personality towards a specific pattern of development. And the role we get to play is always the one which demands those tendencies or qualities from us which are either deficient in our personality or we haven't yet completely learnt to bring out in our behaviour. But when these qualities do become a part of our active behaviour, we attain a more balanced personality.

From this, we can conclude that the universe quite clearly has two intentions behind making a soul acquire a specific role. The first one being that it wants to test the soul. Meaning that it wants to see whether the soul has the strength and ability to imbibe something that is entirely foreign to it or is it unwilling to move out of its comfort zone. While the second being that the universe simply aims to push the soul's limits. This way, it seeks to bring about a certain maturity and balance within the soul. It also aims to break the soul's set conditioning and help expand its vision and experience of the self by enabling the soul to explore a new kind of behavioural response to life. Most importantly, the universe does all this so that the soul can evolve to a higher level.

Therefore, what the universe expects from each of us is not to merely play out the role but to master the tendencies and the higher qualities that our role is supposed to develop in us. Which brings us to the question: How does one actually imbibe the higher qualities of a given role and make it one's soul personality? The answer is by first understanding what these virtues or qualities are and then using the same repeatedly in everyday life, while playing out that given role! To understand this better, let us look at the two examples given below.

Example 1:

Say, one's primary role in life is that of a woman, which broadly demands being affectionate, loving, caring, compassionate, and nurturing. Therefore, it is by being an embodiment of these specific qualities, by actually making these qualities an integral part of one's behaviour, and by using these virtues in everyday interactions with others that a soul, in the role of a woman, can embed these qualities in its personality. And this essentially is the reason the soul has been assigned the role of a woman, so that it can practise and develop qualities that are necessary to balance, solidify, and enhance its personality.

Example 2:

Let us take the case of a financially successful person. Whenever we see someone prosperous or someone living a luxurious life, we instinctively think that this person is simply meant to live a life of comfort, pleasure, and all the enjoyment that comes with immense wealth. And though it is true that wealthy and affluent people enjoy a good life and that it is a reward for certain good deeds in their previous lifetimes, this is not the only reason why they are born rich. There is a much deeper and bigger reason for it, which many of us do not even consider or think about.

As we have discussed before, the most fundamental reason why a role is assigned to us is to better our soul personality! Therefore, when you see a soul in the role of a rich man or woman, think of his or her true purpose in the context of elevating his or her soul personality. And usually in such cases where a soul is playing the role of someone rich, what it needs to cultivate are traits such as humility, gratitude, compassion, and generosity. As until the same is accomplished or until such tendencies reflect in the behaviour of the soul, the given role will not live out its true purpose and the soul will have to come again, perhaps to tougher lifetimes, in order to learn the lessons and tune in its personality towards the direction the universe has intended for it.

Many of us might have a question here that shouldn't a soul already have certain virtues such as kindness, compassion, and humility in its personality in order to acquire the role of a rich person? In other words, is not being born rich a result of one's goodness, which the universe rewards through abundance?

The answer to this might seem counterintuitive but the fact is that richness and abundance have little to do with the personality of a soul. This is because the law of karma observes our actions and intentions most dispassionately and thus, it returns exactly what we have sent out in the world as energy or as experiences and things. The law deals with things more specifically or mathematically than emotionally or analytically. This means that we receive exactly what we have given out. So, in the case of rich people, it essentially implies wealth.

But a point to note here is that wealth may not always be given out from a place of compassion or humility. There are many occasions when one's acts of kindness would be to make up for certain wrong deeds or for the sake of satisfying one's own ego or for the sake of being recognised and lauded by others. It also could be to gain attention in order to feel powerful. Sometimes, people also give away their wealth or donate to charities to dissolve their own fears and troubles or with the intention to gain good karma. Such acts are again motivated by self-interest and do not make the giver a better person in any way.

In all such scenarios, a soul's karmic balance sheet will reflect a credit of the wealth given away or shared with others, which would eventually qualify this soul to be born rich in another lifetime. But the same does not automatically convert to an entitlement of peace, happiness, power, or fearlessness for the soul. This is because when a soul gives away wealth due to some reason originating in ego or due to fear or desire of some kind, it is not going to receive such positive attributes as these are precisely the attributes that the ego always denies.

It is also true that when a soul acquires a role that entails wealth and affluence, it is a great opportunity for the soul to dissolve its ego. For ego loses its grip when there is true generosity, compassion, humility, and selflessness. These qualities also boost peace, happiness, and power. Also, loss of ego arises when one gives up attachments of any kind and when one does something good, purely for the sake of good.

Therefore, souls that have the privilege of wealth need to introspect a bit deeper. They need to check whether or not they are humble, peaceful, joyful, grateful, confident, compassionate, and fearless. Perhaps, this is the very mandate of their given life, to develop these qualities through the right attitude and action. Perhaps, they need to become rich in spirit as well in order to do greater justice to their role!

Example 3:

There are some souls living a life of isolation and prefer

being by themselves. It could be because they lose interest in organised society or because they are not interested in raising a family or making too many friends. Some of them even choose to renounce the world and remain confined in a private space of their choice.

Whatever the physical means of living a life of isolation, what these reclusive souls have acquired through their human role, is a lifetime, devoted to the self for the sake of inner growth, introspection, self-discovery, self-realisation and spiritual evolution. It is not to feel lonely or depressed for not having much human company around, but to devote themselves to building greater self-awareness by spending more time with the self, spending time in nature or through higher learning, wisdom, healing arts or by simply doing something creative. These souls are here to invest in internalisation, reflection, meditation and inner advancement.

The silence and peace in their lives are not there to make them feel lonely but to help them be in that ideal atmosphere, where they can listen and understand the true wisdom of life as well as can focus and reflect on the self.

It is also possible that their past may have been filled with too much noise and distractions, due to which they neglected the self for far too long. Their present life of isolation could therefore be a means to refuel their peace, silence, sense of self-sufficiency, independence, and inner well-being.

Example 4:

Then there are roles that entail a greater level of suffering. There could be various reasons why certain souls might need to undertake such a role but it is mostly because it is only through such roles that these souls can develop inner powers, endurance, acceptance, forgiveness, patience, courage, and spiritual strength. In other words, the purpose of suffering here is to push them towards developing these qualities and thereby transforming them and empowering their personality.

The important point to remember here is that even though, we often think of suffering as something that destroys us mentally, emotionally and at times, even physically, its real aim is to empower us with inner resilience, humility, intuitive intelligence, and spiritual strength. And it does so by driving us towards greater self-awareness.

Another reason why some souls acquire a role that comes with a greater share of suffering is that they have chosen to settle a sizable chunk of karmic debts in a single lifetime. Hence, this way they expedite their journey to spiritual growth and evolution. In such cases, suffering not just helps them undergo a kind of karmic cleansing but also purifies them.

Example 5:

There are many souls essaying the role of the bread earner in a family. The purpose of this role is not to enable one to master the art of making money and simply provide for others but to develop into a person who is selfless, resourceful, dutiful, responsible, and benevolent. Such qualities may be absent or not well developed in souls who acquire this particular role.

Chapter 11

IMPORTANCE OF PLAYING OUR ROLE WELL

There is absolutely no denying the fact that each one of us on this planet has been assigned the most suitable role in our given lifetime. And regardless of the nature of the role and its demands, our real aim should be to progress and be the best at our given role. We also need to understand that our role is a mere vehicle that takes us from one end to another. For we are all energy beings and while our bodies carry us from one end of life to another, it is only through our spiritual or our energy form that we control everything including our body, mind, and actions. And on this very control depends our ultimate growth or decline as a soul. Meaning that if we, as souls or as energy beings, execute our role in a manner that helps us infuse more power into our soul psyche, then it reflects our evolution and growth as a being. Also, if we can play our role in a way that helps us dissolve a considerable amount of accumulated karma then we achieve the higher purpose of our role. Or if we can mature our understanding of the self, others, and life, then again it reflects evolution and growth attained through the role.

However, if we fail to harmonise with the role or we stay clueless about the greater purpose of the role in our journey or while playing the role, we lose our powers and do not achieve the necessary maturity, then we waste this wonderful opportunity to evolve as a being. Not only that but when we fail to align ourselves with the purpose of our role, we tend to create greater confusion in our soul psyche. This confusion arises due to our unwillingness to surrender to the requirements of the role, to change, be flexible, and go with the flow. And this happens when we stay driven by a consciousness controlled by the ego.

But what is ego? Simply put, ego is our accumulated fears, insecurities, body-conscious conditioning, and attachments, all put together. Also, it loves familiarity and is attached to what it believes is right. It teaches us resistance towards life and not acceptance of life. It makes one reject anything that's out of one's familiarity and comfort zone; basically, anything that makes one push their own limitations and boundaries. It makes us averse to flexibility, adaptability, and change; three things that make us do well in our acquired role. And when we don't challenge the dictates of the ego, we are bound to stagnate and fail at our true purpose, which is soul growth! This is the reason why it is extremely vital that we understand ego and learn to oppose it in order to derive maximum growth through our assigned role.

We can see why it is important to overcome ego and do our best in our current role. Here are some ways that encapsulate how you can achieve this.

1. Understand the purpose of the role without any bias. Understand what it wants you to invest mentally, emotionally, and physically.
2. Assess if there are any changes needed in your personality to honour the demands of your role and make that change a priority.

3. If the role challenges you to be what you're not, and if that means changing for the better, then do whatever it takes to bring about that change.
4. Should the ego interfere and create conflict with the role, then don't challenge the role; instead, challenge the ego by leading your life with higher self-awareness and by being an observer of your mind because it's our conditioned mind that is often the voice of the ego.
5. Trust the role and invest positivity in it, give it good energy, and support it.
6. Do not create disharmony with the role by complaining about it or by questioning its value in your life.
7. Should you ever get misaligned with your role and its requirements, make the necessary shift to create a better connection. Do not create doubts, fear, or negativity. This will help you regain your true path and help you go about your role with the right consciousness.
8. Make steady progress. Even the smallest change that a role can influence within your personality is substantial.
9. Regardless of how much you grow or how many new and positive tendencies you acquire, continue integrating these tendencies in your personality by constantly using them or by reflecting them in your behaviour. That's how you'll develop and strengthen your inner personality.
10. Don't compare with other people's roles. Believe that what you have acquired is necessary for the self and therefore, it is the best.

Chapter 12

LEARNING THROUGH OTHER PEOPLE

Surely, we all have come across people whose behaviour we find hard to approve. Does this not happen in our closest relationships, when people close to us—our parents, spouse, sibling, children, or even friends—start behaving in a way that invokes a deep sense of rejection within us, a sense of uneasiness and utmost dislike? The fact is that some people can become so discomforting that it can compel us to create safe mental and emotional boundaries and at times, even walk out of a relationship, especially when it begins to impact us mentally, emotionally, and physically.

There can also be a scenario where everyone else around us may be fine with a certain person and his/her behaviour but only we tend to reject that specific individual's mannerisms. The same can happen within a family or even within a close circle of friends where it is not necessary that whom we dislike is also disliked by everyone else. What this reflects is the fact that the response one person evokes in another is purely subjective as each individual has a specific outlook, threshold, preferences, and their own level of comfort and discomfort with others. It all depends on one's personal capacity and soul personality.

A point to note here is that even though we may vehemently dislike and reject someone, it's not so much them but the way they are that invokes our disapproval. In other words, we never quite reject an individual; we only reject their tendencies. Because the moment they show some positive change, things tend to get better and sanity is restored in relationships.

Now let us look at some important questions that arise from this phenomenon.

- What is it that creates so much disturbance within us that we need to set emotional or physical boundaries with someone?
- What sort of discomfort makes us distance the self from someone, who may not be disliked by others or even be liked and accepted by others?
- When we reject someone's behaviour, do we actually reject something that resonates too personally with us because, at some point, it may have been a part of our own psyche?
- Could it be something else like karma or a shared past that causes this discomfort?

Before delving into these questions, it is important to understand the simple fact that as souls we are all here to learn, evolve, and attain maturity and balance. Our birth brings us to this school called life where the actual learning and education happen through our relationships as they mature us through a myriad of experiences. And in relationships, we are connected to only those people or we get involved in a relationship with only those people, who are here to teach us something about the self, something that we need to learn, something that we need to adopt or reject! And that really is the true purpose of all relationships in our lives.

Come to think of it, why would we choose a certain set of souls only, as our family, friends, neighbours, co-workers, and even acquaintances? Yes, there is a certain karmic payback that we owe towards them but that alone is not the only reason why they are in our lives. The primary reason why we have them in our lives is that we have to learn something about the self from them or in other words, become more self-aware. And the same can also be said for them. That's why we are in these relationships.

It is through our relationships that we experience everything (love, happiness, sorrow, pain, hurt, compassion, selflessness, fulfilment, etc.) which, in turn, teaches us so much about our own state of being which includes 'How are we as a person?', 'What is it that we lack?' and 'What are our strengths?' Hence, we can say that our emotions, our feelings, our thoughts, our conditioning, and even our consciousness are all majorly developed by our relationships.

Without relationships, we cannot really develop or understand the self better. Without relationships, we cannot progress as a soul. Without relationships, we cannot understand what adds to our inner power and what takes the same away! And only when we see others (specifically, those close to us) playing their part, can we understand soul behaviour and soul tendencies and learn the correct way of being. This is how relationships teach us something more about the self and help us evolve by accepting something healthy and by rejecting what is harmful vis a vis soul personality.

So, coming back to the question that why we feel extreme revulsion towards certain people, we can see now that it is because they remind us of something about our own self and this is the reason why we tend to instinctively dismiss such people. To be more precise, we can say that the reason we have a strong reaction to their behaviour is because it invokes some unresolved emotions and tendencies in us that we now need to drop altogether. Tendencies that are ego driven and rob us of our ultimate power. Therefore, a person whose tendencies or behaviour we find uncomfortable is in our life to make us a better being. After all, what meets stiff resistance in us has been a part of our own personality. Otherwise, how would we know how damaging and wrong it is?

For example, let's say that we are uncomfortable with someone who is very aggressive, volatile, and short-tempered. And each time this person gets into a pattern of behaviour which reflects anger, our own inner mechanism starts revolting and we feel so disturbed that we wish to move away from the situation as well as the person. Now, we may have a few other people around us who may be closely connected to this person but they may seem fine and stable while confronting the emotion of anger. Some can even pass it off as normal. But we might find this totally unacceptable and may feel such extreme uneasiness that we may either object to this anger or simply walk away. And all this while, we would be experiencing the same anger in us.

Now clearly, anger is not such a pleasant emotion. It has a painful force and creates extreme unpleasantness, discomfort, and turbulence. Therefore, when a soul gives an emotional response to anger, it shows that it has definitely dealt with anger before. Such a soul may have either battled anger before or may have suffered due to internal anger and so, it understands the enormity of the damage anger can cause and as a result, the soul has become sensitive to the emotion.

So, if we have a strong response against anger, this goes to show that we have experienced such extreme anger in the past and that there is a recording of it in our soul memory that plays out each time someone around us gets angry. But if someone was to tell us what anger is in mere words, we would only have a superficial understanding of the same. Yet, when we experience anger within, when it is an unresolved part of our own tendencies and soul personality, when we have to deal with it or have dealt with it for a fair amount of time, only then would we develop a mental and emotional response to it. This response gets stored in our soul memory and plays out each time we face any kind of anger.

For that matter, even something like depression, nervousness, and anxiety isn't caused by a specific event in life. Rather, they are simply triggered because unless they are a part of our soul recordings, unless they have been a part of our experience over several lifetimes, they cannot be so deeply embedded in our inner personality and cannot become damaging.

An important thing to note here is that the thing which triggers or activates these emotions in us is just a stimulus. The same logic applies to our approval of human behaviour and our appreciation and liking for someone's attitude. Because what we like or approve is often what we need to adopt and make it an integral part of our personality. Therefore, someone's behaviour is only meant to firm up our own learning, either in favour or against a specific tendency. And in this rejection or acceptance lies our lesson, our understanding, and our shift from immaturity to growth! It is like the universe is cementing something in our consciousness and making us understand a precious lesson so that we either completely do away or develop a particular tendency for good.

The important thing to realise here is that we are constantly learning through roles around us and what we accept or reject in people does not have much to do with them but our own self! It is our own self that gets educated, enlightened, and improved in the course of our interactions with others. After all, it is not a mere superficial understanding that can help us learn our precious lessons. The same will have to be let in through the emotional route, so that they settle down deep into our psyche and manifest through the being.

Chapter 13
SOUL TRUTH

Our past influences our present. Our present influences the future, which becomes our present at some point and subsequently becomes our past as well. And like this, we move from one life or life experience to another, ever connected to our past and ever driven by the law of cause and effect.

It is through this amazing interplay of the past, present, and future that a soul goes through its unique set of experiences, learns its lessons, reworks its tendencies, and advances towards evolution, which is its ultimate goal. However, those who consider the past or to be more precise, past life, a mere illusion and the present as the only reality need to align with a deeper thought process.

Yes, the present is all that may be in our hands, but the past too is important in the context of the present. This is because the past is the reason why we are who we are and what we are going through in the present! So, first, let us just accept that we all have past lives and that these past lives have a solid connection with our present truth. After all, given the vast variety of souls on the planet, given their exceptionally unique personalities and distinguishing traits, their distinct leanings, preferences, ideologies, concepts, choices, behaviour, hopes and wishes, and the difference in their physical, emotional, mental, intellectual, social, and economic realities, it would be naive to think that people are merely a creation of the moment.

It is too convenient to assume that who we are is purely out of coincidence or even choice for that matter. Some people also subscribe to the belief that we are what we are, as a result of our present life only. They hold responsible factors such as our childhood, our growing years, the situations, events and circumstances of our present life, and our economic, social, cultural, and family environments for who we are and what we experience in a given life. No doubt, this does have a role to play in shaping our personality, but then, there are scores of instances where from negative situations, circumstances, events, and environment, a soul has emerged positive and clean and has actually done things for the good of humanity. There are instances where respectable families, with the most privileged, happy, comfortable, and favourable environments have had the misfortune of having a child grow up and become a criminal, an addict, or even someone who ends up doing a complete disservice to the self, the society, and to the privileges he or she was born with.

In other words, we have seen good people emerge from bad environments and bad people emerge from the best possible environments. We have seen people operating with dishonesty despite the lessons regarding honesty that were taught to them while growing up. And we have seen people subscribe to higher values, despite being fed the psychology of thieves in their growing years.

We have seen some stunning talents and abilities surface at a tender age without any formal training or education. We have also seen phobias and fears in strong and physically healthy people, the source of which cannot be traced to the immediate past or to their genetics. In fact, we have also seen diseases and defects with just no logical or substantial cause connected to the present life's past.

Thus, we can see through numerous examples that the present life has little bearing on a soul's eventual reality. And how does one explain this strange but observable fact of polarities and the scores of inexplicable realities without connecting them to a journey much longer? A journey that encompasses past lifetimes and traces a soul's history, its mannerisms, experiences, priorities, and actions that have a strong hold on its psyche, which, in turn, attracts the set of experiences and life paths that the soul must live through its present human form. The truth is that our past life patterns do get recorded in our subconscious memory and can be accessed either through past life regression techniques or through deep meditative practices. In fact, even the science of astrology, when applied with the right intent, can deliver this truth to us. After all, what is a birth chart but a blueprint of our past life thoughts and actions, detailing the theory of cause and effect as relevant to us individually. In fact, the ancient science of astrology can reveal a lot more. It can also reveal what motivates a soul, how its mind and intelligence operate, what level of wisdom it has gained, and what are its karmic balances. It can also reveal what a soul has accomplished in past lives, its default patterns, and even the direction it chose pre-birth. In fact, the entire science of astrology and horoscope is based on past life patterns and their impact on a soul's present reality.

Therefore, how can we say that there is no past? How can we deny the fact that we all live the life that we live for a bigger reason than we probably know? Is it not better to accept that there are some things which the universe keeps hidden from us for our own good? However, it still does give us an intuitive sense of the same in order to push us towards our own evolution and maturity!

The fact is that our conscious memory has very little information and because it remains active majority of the time (it is always active except in deep sleep), the subconscious is hardly accessed. But there is a whole lot of recorded information in the subconscious, which a soul carries along through lifetimes. And it is this very recording, which is nothing but the truth of a soul's karmas and tendencies, that together make a soul respond to life in the way it does in the present moment. Or we can say that it is this energy of past karmic actions and tendencies that attracts the soul's present-lifetime experiences, lessons, struggles, and triumphs as well as its karmic mandate.

Therefore, the role that a soul plays is only a manifestation of this accumulated energy and perhaps, a physical representation of an effect that emerges from a past cause. A cause that every soul should trace in order to successfully play its present life role and achieve its higher purpose in life. A purpose that aims to help the soul ascend to its higher self by dissolving karmas and tendencies that weigh down its growth prospects.

SECTION 2

In the next few chapters of this book, we will try to broadly identify and understand some individual soul types and get an expanded view of what makes them who they are. The categories mentioned here will cover the predominant characteristics and personality traits of each soul type in that category as well as their karmic mandate or their pending karma towards their own growth and well-being.

Also, in this section, the concept of karmic mandates is very important to understand and honour because they not only help a soul regain its lost powers but also contribute to the mental, emotional, psychological, and spiritual evolution of the soul. Something that cannot be achieved unless the karmic mandate of a given life is fully honoured.

Do note that individually, these souls could be a blend of different tendencies but it's their true personality or their more dominating tendency is what that sets them as who they are. And it is this dominating tendency that drives a majority of their thoughts, feelings, actions as well as their approach to life which then sets the tone of their destiny and explains why it is so important to uncover this tendency and get a logical sense of one's truth!

The readers can also delve deeper into their own habits, behaviour, and personality traits to identify with a particular category. And should they feel they belong to a particular type or a combination of categories, then adhering to the karmic mandate of their present life as mentioned under each soul type would prove beneficial for them.

The idea here is to provide the necessary guidance that can help individuals identify and take appropriate steps to dissolve their darker and heavier patterns of behaviour. Patterns that are responsible for creating more karmic bondage, spiritual degeneration, and difficulties in various aspects of life. The information provided in this section will help the readers identify and enhance healthier patterns to achieve greater growth and well-being.

So, if one can pick the pieces of their own puzzle and view the complete picture and thereby understand why they are who they are, it would be a milestone in their individual journey.

Chapter 14

WISE SOULS

Wisdom is not something that is gained through study or learning; it is something that is gained through experience, which, in turn, makes us understand the true meaning of life. And once acquired, wisdom gets reflected not just in words but also in one's behaviour and attitude towards life, in the way one conducts the self, and in one's choices and priorities in life. Thus, we can say that wisdom has a more profound meaning and implication than what the majority broadly understands.

A wise soul most definitely carries many lifetimes of experiences that have helped it develop a deeper understanding of life, stability of mind, and astuteness of the intellect, which rarely fails in guiding the soul towards what is right.

A point to note here is that we all are capable of being wise and developing wisdom, which is necessary for a successful and wholesome experience of life. Success in the given context is a combination of sensible decisions, effective actions, egoless behaviour, and all that brings about one's mental, emotional, and spiritual growth. And this kind of success is the fruit of wisdom.

But despite being capable of equal wisdom, we are never at an equal level. This is because we all have unique journeys as souls, and we all travel and grow at a different pace. Also, our individual journeys, comprising various experiences, can be divided into two categories:

- A journey which forces us to develop a sense of higher wisdom, owing to the kind of experiences we encounter and endure.
- A journey with experiences that have a neutral influence on us. In other words, experiences countered in this specific journey do not push us towards soul searching and developing a deeper understanding of life.

And on closer observation, we will find that souls who seem to have successfully imbibed wisdom, are the ones who, in their previous incarnations, have had the experiences that brought along some level of learning and growth. Experiences that came with a sense of awakening and brought along a deeper understanding of the self and life as a whole. It is possible that these experiences were intense, yet liberating and helped these souls grasp the bigger picture and evolve to a new level of maturity.

So, these are souls who have a far more detached take on life and all its aspects. They are less emotionally triggered and inclined towards developing their higher self. Perhaps, it was their tough lives in the past that compelled them to look within and work on the self in order to generate a better experience. It also could be their own urge, arising from a feeling of being satiated with worldly things, which led them towards soul searching and a desire for enlightenment. In short, these are souls who have come into the present life with higher learning from their previous lives, which may have been either forced by circumstances or may have been absorbed out of one's own necessity for self-realisation and growth. And this higher learning has resulted in the purification of their mind, emotions, and intellect, helping them mature and turn wiser.

Another factor is that true wisdom originates from one's own intuitive mind and it is highly likely that wise souls have invested time in developing their intuitive ability through meditative practices and spiritual learning in their previous lives.

Wise souls can be broadly identified as those who have this rare capacity to live life with a higher level of acceptance and deal with situations with greater maturity. They are also less emotional and more realistic about things and therefore, can endure any life situation with equanimity and resilience. One could say that wise souls give a more balanced response to life as they do not get carried away in the good and bad that they encounter.

Wise souls follow higher principles, lead lives free from dogmas, conventions, superstition, and fear, and are able to strike the right balance between the material and spiritual life. In short, these are souls that are essentially driven by the voice of their conscience. And all these attributes have their foundation in their past lives where they were either pushed by circumstances or it was their free will that helped them grasp the true meaning and purpose of life.

This also brings us to another interesting fact. Wise souls have settled a bigger part of their karmic debts. This is because true wisdom can only be attained once one is able to reduce the burden of debts and go beyond the karmic suffering, which tends to keep one entangled in worldly duties and obligations in ways that leave no time or desire for a deeper understanding of life. Having too much of karmic debts means that one needs to focus on paying them back.

Therefore, souls who can turn inward and focus on the self with the aim of achieving enlightenment and growth are the ones with relatively lesser karmic accounts to settle. Of course, while settling our karmic debts, many souls do tend to learn and mature but ultimate wisdom is delivered only when one has the will and the time to focus on the self with a desire for self-improvement. Also, any learning that comes through our karmic settlement translates into wisdom only if one has developed a certain level of humility. Humility helps convert resistance to wisdom and acceptance. And one can develop humility only by going through a wide range of experiences that instil maturity and clear out a major karmic burden.

Wise souls are rich in such experiences and so, their humility is well developed. They are the ones who have already passed their set of trials and learnt their karmic lessons which naturally helped them mature and embark on a journey to self-exploration and growth. The thing that brings them into their present birth is their keenness to ascend spiritually, as achieving wisdom or a sense of awakening is the first step to the real evolution of every soul. So, for the wise souls, what comes next is a responsibility to help and guide other souls who may still be in oblivion and also continue their own learning in the process.

The Karmic Mandates for Wise Souls

These are the three essential present-life karmic mandates for wise souls:

1. **Their own spiritual advancement**

   With the seed of awakening sown in their past lives, wise souls now come with a karmic mandate to advance spiritually and restore their spiritual powers which get depleted while settling a bigger burden of karma. And regaining these powers is necessary for their own spiritual growth and overall well-being.

Spiritual advancement for wise souls comes with the prospect of enlightenment and growth. So, from a state of awakening, these souls now need to become enlightened and operate their life with higher self-awareness. They are here to understand and decode the mystical and spiritual secrets through subjects that only a few can grasp. Also, life will give these souls the kind of opportunities and experiences which will help them refine their wisdom.

The primary mandate for these souls is the expansion of consciousness, which is something that naturally starts at awakening. As only after one has awakened, one advances spiritually in various stages, one of which is enlightenment.

2. Helping other souls

Another important karmic mandate for wise souls is to help the unconscious minds find the solutions to their problems and bring to light a more conscious, liberating, and evolved state of being. This helps souls who are in difficulty to enter a positive orbit and understand their own deficiencies. It also inspires them to rise above their limited thought process and conditioning and identify unconscious behaviour patterns.

To honour their present mandate, wise souls need to share their wisdom by creating a piece of work that enlightens those in need of help. The core idea here being that wise souls need to ensure the correct dissemination of wisdom-related information to promote self-awareness. This is because not everyone has the capacity to grasp this information and so, it needs to come from a source that interprets the same correctly and makes it easier for others to make it a way of life.

Another interesting fact that emerges from this is that sharing and guiding others on the path of wisdom helps the one guiding others grow wiser. Because when one shares wisdom, one also opens the doors for new information to come in. And this, in turn, enhances one's own ability to understand the thing being taught.

3. **Balancing the energy of the planet**

Wise souls come with yet another important mandate: to balance the energy of the planet and counter any heaviness or darkness. So, even if their physical presence isn't as noticeable, these souls radiate good energy and positivity, which is necessary to create overall stability and balance in their immediate environment. This can be achieved by interacting with others through an elevated state of being and by consciously choosing to operate through higher consciousness.

Chapter 15
EMOTIONAL SOULS

The main feature of emotional souls is that they usually have an emotional response to life and various situations and events entailed within it. With their sentiments riding high, they can be easily moved to sadness and hurt or to laughter and cheer. They can also oscillate between different emotions and have unpredictable behaviour. Meaning that one moment these souls will be happy, inspired, or enthusiastic, and the next they will be sad, angry, or depressed. They may be short-tempered or volatile but can also forgive easily. In fact, it doesn't take much effort to move emotional souls from one state of mind to another as they are extremely sensitive to situations and people and are completely driven by their feelings, which, in turn, makes them prone to mood swings.

So, as discussed, emotional souls can be intense, tender, highly strung, spirited, gutsy, fiery, and aggressive, depending upon how their feelings are channelled. These souls can also be swayed quite easily as they are impressionable. They are also overly sympathetic and may go all out to help anyone who stirs up their emotions. You may often find them teary-eyed while watching a tragic movie or while listening to a painful narrative. The truth is that there are really no safeguards against their emotional thought process for they think as they feel and that is why these souls can be quite unpredictable. But because they have no restraint on their feelings, they can also be utterly honest, transparent, and often harmless to others as they are easy to read.

Also, with emotions being their key driving force, these souls tend to see everything through the filter of their feelings. Their thoughts, opinions, and decisions are not based on what their head tells them but on how their feelings prompt them or how they interpret a situation for them. So, all their assumptions, all their beliefs, and even their state of being for that matter originate from their feelings.

Due to this reason, emotional souls tend to act impulsively and get carried away, which can be self-destructive as most of their decisions and reactions are not thought through. And should any disappointment or hurt come their way, these souls can sulk and brood to the extent of harming their own peace and stability as they are highly susceptible to self-doubt, insecurity, and negativity. This is something that can be quite damaging for them and their relationships as their feelings are not guided by reasonable logic.

Given the vulnerability of their psyche, emotional souls can be quite possessive and jealous and have extreme emotions towards life as well as towards other people. They usually tend to like or dislike things and have no middle path vis-à-vis their preference. Due to their emotions constantly being in overdrive mode, these souls tend to form opinions easily as they do not feel the necessity to weigh their opinions on a scale of practical logic. Often pushed by the intensity of their feelings, they tend to jump to conclusions and pass judgement easily. Many a time, they miss the bigger picture and ultimately end up feeling defeated or lost, when the reality gets revealed to them.

On the other hand, emotional souls can be extremely passionate and pursue things and even relationships with great drive and intensity. They are easily excitable and reactive because they do not let the intellect participate in the way they behave and operate in life. These souls also think a lot about the past or worry about the future and are often disconnected from the present.

Owing to their high emotional vulnerability, emotional souls tend to take a whole lot of burden on themselves and often think too much, especially after any kind of setback in life. They also overanalyse the results of their actions and can be overly imaginative and suspicious at times. Being constantly driven by feelings also makes them edgy and easily stressed and anxious. Their psyche can easily become overloaded as there is hardly any space between their thoughts, which are triggered by hyperactive feelings.

Though it is easy to see that emotional souls are softhearted and often have the best intentions for everyone, whether they are good and kind towards the self is something that remains questionable. Their attitude can be far more self-destructive instead of self-nourishing. This is bound to happen when one is completely dictated by the mind and the intellect (reasoning) isn't allowed ample participation in decision-making. The mind and the intellect are the greatest powers of each soul, and denying permission to any one of them can mislead a soul and cause grave disappointments in the way it experiences life. Excessive use of the mind and a lack of balance between the mind and the intellect often also results in huge ego in these souls. This ego translates into anger, fear, attachments, insecurity, and all other tendencies which have their foundation in overblown emotions. In fact, it is emotions that make these souls vulnerable to pain that often betrays their inner strength.

Emotional souls have a heavily conditioned mind and they are often, the prisoner of this mind. In fact, it is the constant noise of their mind or the continuous thinking that keeps their emotions energised. Therefore, it may be said that emotional souls need to work on their psychological health. This can be done by balanced participation of the head and the heart or the mind and the intellect. But before we understand their karmic mandate, it is important to tap into the past life experiences of these souls as they can be a predominant cause of their present-day psyche.

It can be said that their excessively active emotional side indicates a past life, which may have been challenging. Perhaps, they may have faced extreme hardships or had experiences that were bitter or emotionally provocative or physically and mentally exhausting. These can include experiences of betrayal or deceit, isolation, disillusionment, abuse, persecution, loss of love or relationship, physical torture, financial turbulence, etc. Basically, challenges that may have been unpredictable, shocking, or difficult to handle and thus, resulted in these souls becoming emotionally vulnerable as well as reactive. Thus, it can be said that emotional souls most likely had a past that included negatively transformative experiences that pushed them towards insecurity, fear, and resistance to life. Tendencies that feed the ego and cause emotional turmoil. After all, when we cannot handle things or when we fail at understanding life and people, we take to excessive emotional thinking, which often is the cause of our inner turmoil.

The instant arousal of emotions in these souls, for any reason whatsoever, is indicative of the fact that they neither had the convenience nor the sense to stop and check their own thought process and behaviour. Perhaps, it can be their difficult karmic dues or the return of past karma which made their mental and physical situation so demanding and all-consuming that these souls neither had the privilege to stop nor the capacity to think beyond their limited scenarios.

The Karmic Mandates for Emotional Souls

These are three essential present-life karmic mandates for emotional souls:

1. **Developing greater self-awareness**

   As discussed earlier, the primary purpose of life for emotional souls is to bring about an internal change and in order to do so, they need to develop greater self-awareness which is one of their key karmic mandates. These souls need to be more attentive to their inner world than the outer and through self-awareness, they need to guide themselves to a more balanced and harmonious state of being. Self-awareness is the key here because only when one is aware of their emotions can they do something about it. In fact, the entire process of inner growth starts with self-awareness. Also, with greater self-awareness, one can get a better grip over their reactions and prevent getting carried away by thoughts or a situation. This is because when we watch our thoughts, their speed reduces and this is something that can help in channelling one's emotions correctly.

   Therefore, emotional souls need to live with constant self-awareness and engage in a more constructive relationship with the self. They need to understand that while the past or perhaps, even the present may be quite difficult, at some point, they need to cross over. They need to stop being a victim of situations, people, and life experiences. And for this, they need to understand the importance of their own self and realise that it is they who make their own life what it is and so, they must remain more alert and careful towards the self.

Self-awareness will also help these souls when life situations become emotionally draining. It will help them stay non-reactive and avoid giving more power to their feelings by not identifying with the very intensity of such feelings, which, in turn, will provide them with much-needed relief and protection.

2. Learning to use the intellect (reasoning/logic)

Emotional souls are here to see life not as a mere emotional experience but as a means to tackle emotional volatility and vulnerability through the influence of greater tact and reasoning.

An important karmic mandate for these souls is to inculcate the habit of being logical. They need to understand that it's a hyperactive mind that leads to hyperactive emotions and so, as soon as the mind goes into overdrive, they need to turn inward and watch the compulsive thought process rather than responding through it. These souls need to let the reasoning of the intellect drive their actions and not allow the prompting of their feelings to make them jump to conclusions. In other words, they need to seek logical reasoning for everything and not just unconsciously flow in a sea of emotions. The compulsive and unconscious patterns of their behaviour need to come under close scrutiny and must be replaced with a more rational and conscious approach.

So, the next time such souls find their emotions being challenged by an outer situation or a person, they need to remind themselves about not giving in. They need to stop getting sucked into their own emotional currents and simply avoid giving a reaction or forming an opinion in that very moment.

Next, they need to involve their intellect towards understanding the situation more logically and impartially. Although initially, it may be hard for them to decipher what their intellect is telling them because they have kept the intellect dormant or passive for a long while. But with time, their logical side will become more attuned and their old patterns will begin to dissolve. This way, their intellect will start working in tandem with their mind.

3. **Live consciously and responsibly**

Emotional souls need to realise that their overbearing emotional side leads to an unhealthy psyche, lack of physical health, and a sense of low self-esteem, which is ego. They also need to understand that the universe will continue responding to their energy and will keep returning what they send out, until these souls change the very nature of their response to life. In order to achieve this, they need to live more consciously and responsibly. And until they do so, situations that bother them or take a toll on their emotions will keep repeating and draining their energy.

So, when these difficult situations arise, emotional souls must learn to simply observe them and not absorb them as it leads to an emotional response. Also, living life consciously and responsibly entails that these souls see situations and people as an observer rather than the judge or the jury. They mustn't label situations and people in any way (neither good nor bad) and simply learn to observe them sans judgement. This will definitely help conserve energy and maintain a balance of emotions.

Another factor that contributes to conscious living is leading a baggage-free life. So, these souls need to release all the hard feelings and hurt that they carry with them. This is an important step to securing good emotional health.

Then there's the practice of stillness. Emotional souls need to train their mind to slow down when needed. This means that from time to time, these souls need to create space within. Meaning, they need to watch their thoughts to the point that their thoughts slow down and eventually stop. And once thinking ceases, even if it is for a minute or a few seconds, space gets created in one's mind. This space promotes inner peace and balance as well as leads to creative thinking.

A part of conscious living also mandates that these souls think positive thoughts. Because when one thinks positive thoughts, one thinks less, and when one thinks negative thoughts, one thinks more. Subliminally, thinking happens to create something within. The desire of everyone is to create a positive feeling. A feeling that can fill the vacuum within. And when one thinks positive thoughts, one automatically creates a positive feeling. This way the vacuum gets filled easily. This positive feeling can also slow down thinking as one naturally wants to sustain such a feeling.

But when one thinks negative thoughts, the vacuum only gets bigger. This makes one think more in order to fill the vacuum. A vacuum which will always grow bigger till one makes the conscious effort to change the quality of one's thoughts.

Chapter 16

SUFFERING SOULS

As long as a soul is living a human life, it is inevitable that it will experience some sort of pain, hurt, and grief at one point or another. These feelings are probably as inevitable as feelings of joy, comfort, and cheer, which again are an integral part of a soul's human journey.

The experiences of hurt, pain, and grief occur due to physical, mental, and material hardships or due to events and situations that are demanding and beyond one's control. Even though the magnitude of their impact may vary from soul to soul, what is certain is that hurt, pain, and grief are an unavoidable reality for everyone! Yet, it is totally up to the soul's own will to either hold on to the hurt and convert it into long-lasting suffering or simply let it go. Let us analyse this point further.

Suffering is created when we choose to hold on to any hurt, pain, or grief, even after the cause or the source of their trigger is long gone. Meaning, suffering only occurs when the experience of an unfortunate event or scenario remains with us as a painful memory for too long or more precisely, when that sensation is allowed to permeate the subconscious. And it is quite possible that we may forget the exact event which caused the hurt or grief, but their sensation is something that may stay with us and cause suffering long after.

Another point to understand here is that suffering can manifest differently in different people. It can take the form of fears, deep insecurities, anxiety, depression, phobia, delusions, lack of contentment, low self-esteem, paranoia, a sense of insufficiency, and in certain cases, even mistrust and suspicion. These tendencies can have a damaging effect on the soul's psyche, relationships, health, and well-being.

Another point to note here is that suffering is different from struggling as one can suffer, even when one does not need to. For example, one can suffer from too much wealth as well as the lack of it. One can suffer in happiness as well as in misery. One can suffer in pain and even in its absence. One can suffer in comfort as well as in discomfort. And one can suffer in loss and even without it. Thus, we can see that external events or circumstances may not necessarily be the triggers to our internal suffering. In other words, if we choose to hold on to any kind of disturbing feeling or memory for long, we can suffer in even the best of circumstances.

Also, sometimes minor difficulties can simply become an excuse to surface our already existing mental, emotional, or spiritual agony. And this kind of suffering arises from a deep disorder in a soul's personality or from unaddressed trauma in the soul's memory. That is, suffering can be said to be self-imposed or self-inflicted misery because it stems from one's inability to let go of feelings attached to events that are long over.

On the other hand, when one is struggling, he or she may not necessarily have the option of coming out of it. The struggle could be financial or pertaining to relationships, health, etc. But in suffering, there is always a way out, there is always a choice to correct one's state of mind by taking charge of one's inner well-being.

So, we can conclude that suffering is a mental, emotional, or psychological state, which is often self-created and to emerge out of it, an enormous amount of awareness is needed. For when we remain unconscious of our own emotions and feelings, when we cannot stop our train of thoughts from constantly moving in a negative direction, we suffer. Or when we cling to feelings that are emotionally depleting and stay tuned to the noise in our mind, we suffer. And as long as we stay entangled in our own mental and emotional deceptions, we will continue to suffer.

Even in the case of physical pain or say, a personal loss, one has the choice to experience the pain and grief to a point and then come out of it in order to move on. The other choice is to continue prolonging the experience of pain and grief, which, in turn, prolongs suffering. It all depends on the way one approaches life and the mental strength one has to accept the truth and move on. Though again, the ability and the power of the mind are all that matter here as the intellect always knows that there is no point in holding on to any kind of pain. But it is the mind which makes all the noise and most often stops us from letting go of suffering.

Here, we once again need to emphasise that suffering is never due to the various situations or events in life. These can be the triggers, but people who suffer are often victims of their own psyche or deficiencies in their soul personality. The more astonishing fact is that sometimes, people suffer for no reason at all. And their inner state of suffering will often reveal itself in complaints, criticism, lack of contentment, unhappiness, and lack of trust, which remains constant and at most times, unreasonable.

People can be in healthy relationships and still feel that something is missing and keep complaining about their loved ones. Then there are people who may have a good job and a great working environment and yet, they continue to hanker for more. There are also people who have an opulent life and still they do not feel satisfied with what they have. Such souls will always have something or the other to lament about and criticise. And this way, they can suffer endlessly!

The fact is that not only in their current lifetime, but these souls have shown no inclination to move from the poverty of their minds to prosperity and a sense of abundance in their previous lifetimes as well. They have dwelled in their state of suffering for far too long and have therefore developed a false sense of security and comfort in being ever dissatisfied, ever complaining, brooding, and grieving. And when this becomes a subtle and dangerous habit, it makes them oblivious to self-examination, reflection, and change. Therefore, if we investigate the psyche of such souls, we will find a lot of damage caused due to their own ignorance towards a negative and draining pattern of thoughts, feelings, and emotions.

So, why the psyche of suffering souls behaves the way it does? On closer inspection, we find that it is probably due to some terrible event or some untoward experience in their past life, which struck them unaware, unprepared, and unguarded, went on to impact their feelings in a way that they lost faith in life and in people, or lost their confidence and their sense of comfort, security, and optimism which, in turn, gave way to fear, doubts, insecurity, unhappiness, dissatisfaction, and despair. The sensation of their bitter experience continues to haunt them and govern their feelings and because of this, these souls continue to suffer.

Certainly, there is a definite history that these souls need to take into consideration. But the thing that they need to understand is that no matter how ugly or difficult an experience of life may be, it only happens to make us wiser. It happens to rid us of our negative karma and set us free from the energy of our own actions. The kind of energy that tends to weigh us down and impedes our growth.

It is also true that the event or experience which changed the psyche of suffering souls may have actually occurred to inspire some sort of wisdom in them or help them learn a precious lesson necessary for their spiritual growth. For every challenging event of life comes with its set of learning. Even if it is something excruciating, it comes with lessons that have the ability to make us wiser. But the fact that these souls chose suffering over learning is the reason for who they are and where they are today. For learning is always the end of suffering or one can say, learning helps one avoid suffering as it matures a soul.

But those who resist such learning fall into the trap of suffering. Such souls deny attention and treatment to their own mental and emotional scars by constantly thinking, feeling, and behaving like the one at the receiving end of most negativity. It is hard to not notice their deep-rooted pessimism and make them believe that the world is indeed a good place. And since they continue dwelling in their deeply conditioned self, such souls soon become detached from the present and this essentially is the primary cause of their state of being. Their overblown ego, nurtured through the emotions of fear, anxiety, doubt, negativity and attachment, is yet another reason for suffering.

The Karmic Mandates for Suffering Souls

These are three essential present-life karmic mandates for suffering souls:

1. **Living in the present**

   The most important karmic mandate for suffering souls is to develop the ability to live in the present. In fact, once these souls start being attentive to their life in the present moment and fully surrender to what the present moment has to offer, it will be hard for them to go by the diktats of their conditioned self.

The same can be done by training the mind to focus on the present moment. This way, they can align with the present moment and give their energy to all that there is in 'now', regardless of whether there is silence or noise or even discomfort. These people need to experience the same to the fullest. They can also take up activities that help to stay present. Sporting activities, hiking, gardening, driving and even yoga and fitness training can be a good way to bring presence into one's life.

And once being present becomes a habit, it will not just break their conditioning but will also help them look at life differently. It will restore their positivity and create a sense of newness.

2. **Learning to think and feel differently**

Based on our discussion before, what suffering souls haven't paid attention to in the past is learning. Even though what they suffered did make them settle heavy karmic debts but what was missed in their prior journey was learning something vital. For if learning is resisted, it only gives more strength to the ego.

So, with all their unaddressed fears, insecurities, and uneasiness, which stem from the ego, suffering souls need to take refuge in learning. They need to open up to a new way of thinking and exploring life and for that, they need to associate with some form of higher learning. This can be spiritual wisdom, psychology, philosophy, or just a mix of all relevant subjects that can help these souls better understand the self. Though if this is not possible, then seeking direct counselling can also help them learn a lot about the self and get rid of their unwanted baggage.

All in all, suffering souls need to develop a new way of thinking and feeling. And for that, they need guidance that helps them gain perspective as well as the ability to view things as they are. This, in turn, will help these souls practice detachment from their own suffering and all external influences that trigger and fuel their suffering!

3. Inner transformation

It is true that we all have the ability to not let our fears, insecurities, pain, hurt, or any kind of negative emotion turn into suffering. For suffering becomes our nature when we allow our negative feelings or emotions to start dictating our thoughts. But if we can develop self-awareness, self-control, and self-discipline regarding the slightest negativity that we feel within and check our thoughts from time to time or intentionally replace negative thoughts with positive ones, we can undoubtedly break the pattern of suffering. This indeed can bring about the inner transformation that's necessary for souls with a tendency to suffer.

Thus, we can conclude that inner transformation is a clear mandate for suffering souls and they are here to become wiser, more positive, and calmer. From feeling like a victim to being in complete control of their life and not having any preconceived notions about anything is what transformation is all about. And such transformation can only occur when these souls can generate the necessary self-awareness and make new learnings and wisdom an integral part of their being.

Chapter 17
HAPPY SOULS

Happiness is a tendency and also a natural state for each one of us. Natural because we all like to be happy and are comfortable being happy. However, not every soul is able to operate through this tendency and some even seek happiness outside of them, i.e., through an external source, person, event, situation, object, achievement, etc. But happiness is an innate quality, and it can be only accessed within the dimensions of our own mind and spirit. External things can sometimes act as a stimulus to our happiness but such happiness doesn't last for long. It's just the icing on the cake and not the cake itself. For happiness is a feeling within and a tendency that needs to be realised and made active. And only some special souls have the ability and the power to do that. They are able to access their inner happiness and make it a way of life.

But what is it that makes it so easy for happy souls to access a dimension, which others desperately seek or even struggle to connect with? To answer this question, let us first understand the nature of happy souls. These are souls who come across as cheerful, joyful, secure, light, and carefree, with or without any external reason contributing to their rare and powerful state. For it is true that we do not really need a reason to be happy and no effort is needed to create happiness for the self. We do not need someone or something to make us happy because we already have happiness as a soul tendency which is a part of our natural spiritual power.

Something that can be understood by checking our own state of being. For isn't it true that there are times when we can be happy for no reason at all and sometimes, even the best of situations cannot make us as happy as we should be? It happens because there are times when we can fully access our internal happiness and times when our mind becomes so clouded that we either seek happiness from an external source or are unable to connect with our own happiness in situations when we should ideally be happy.

But when it comes to happy souls, they have the power to process things in a way that helps them easily access their inner happiness and operate life through this tendency. They not just prioritise their happiness but also let it permeate into their feelings. And this is one rare ability which helps these souls remain in a state of joy at most times.

As mentioned earlier, most of us often rely on external triggers when it comes to happiness. But there are some people who can be happy for no particular reason. Even when things around them go south, they still manage to remain happy. To understand this phenomenon, we will have to look into the nature of human beings.

As human beings, we have a range of emotions, or what we also call tendencies, within us. We have accumulated these tendencies over various lifetimes owing to our behaviour in different life situations and experiences. So, how we have responded to life is who we have become. Our state of happiness also results from the same. For if we chose to respond correctly by using the right tendency and emotion, it will definitely save us from a lot of complications, both outside and within. In such a scenario, our inner state would remain empowered and our happiness would remain unhindered.

Our response to life also determines how much of our inherent sense, wisdom, and spiritual powers we have managed to retain and if we are now capable of using the same in order to tap into the right tendency. Usually, if our mind and intellect are working in tandem or if we are operating out of self-awareness, we can manage to tap into and operate through the right tendency, which includes happiness as well. But then there are also times when we are not able to generate the same because we are not in the right frame of mind or we do not have harmony of the mind and intellect. Usually, when the mind is the dominant force and the intellect is subdued, there is too much noise and thinking happening. This noise is often of low-quality thoughts, which occur too fast and create heaviness in one's feelings. One can also feel edgy and anxious during such times. And it is this heaviness that becomes the roadblock to accessing happiness.

Such is not the pattern of happy souls and we can conclude that these souls have done something right to be where they are! The fact that they have managed to retain their inner powers and their ability to access the right tendencies is not just extraordinary but also a combination of certain healthy factors. And one such factor is karma.

Our balance of karmic debts has a great influence on the way we feel. For feelings are the window to our soul. This is also why some people can smile in misery and that's because their soul is cheerful, i.e., their pending karmas are light. On the other hand, some people complain even in comfort and that's because their soul is in darkness, i.e., their pending karmas are heavy.

Happy souls have a low burden of karma and their karmic record is pretty straight and clean which means there is no regret, remorse, or suffering within and due to this, their energy remains positive and light. This gives them the rare ability to balance their mind (emotions) and intellect (reasoning) and manage the correct response to life.

A good karmic record plays a big part here because when our karma is clean and our own energy positive, we do not attract any dark or heavy energy or experience towards us. And good, clean karma also amounts to a clean conscience, high soul power, positive intent, and pure thoughts. All these factors play an important role when it comes to accessing happiness.

So, as discussed, happiness is something that can be found within all of us, just like all other emotions. But which emotion is more predominant in our psyche or in our behaviour depends upon the state of our conscience and subconscious mind. The subconscious mind is a storehouse of deeds, experiences, thoughts, feelings, and emotions, which we have accumulated over many lifetimes and the quality of this accumulation determines our inner state.

Therefore, a happy soul is very likely a soul with good deeds, noble thoughts, pure intent, and a clean or light subconscious mind. Which, in turn, capacitates their conscious mind to choose happiness over all other emotions as the soul's most predominant trait or tendency. On the contrary, if the subconscious is heavy and if there is a lot of karmic guilt, hurt, and dark thoughts and feelings along with questionable intent in the subconscious memory of the soul, then it becomes difficult for such a soul to choose an emotion as positive and light as happiness. Such a soul usually has a noisy mind and gravitates towards anxiety, fear, sadness, and tense emotions that are in sharp contrast to happiness.

So, we can see why some souls have the power to access happiness and as a result, they remain light and blissful.

Clearly, there is no major burden on their psyche and no major guilt stored in their subconscious memory. Instead, they are driven by a healthy and strong psyche.

Happy souls also have a few other important attributes that support their consistent state of happiness. These include:

- A selfless nature, which is a byproduct of happiness and reflects a secure inner state that further boosts happiness.
- An easy-going approach, which protects them from getting mentally and emotionally tangled up with people and situations, leading to sustained happiness.
- Ability to do a lot more in life because there are hardly any blocks in their energy field.
- A higher intuitive intelligence that can grasp mature and evolved subjects.
- A grateful heart that remains largely appreciative of others and operates through inner abundance.

The Karmic Mandates for Happy Souls

These are the three essential present-life karmic mandates for happy souls:

1. **Working for a higher cause**

   Happy souls have the potential to contribute to the greater good and benefit society at large. This is due to the fact that their selfless temperament makes them ideal for humanitarian, social, and environmental causes. Thus, we can infer that one of the important karmic mandates for happy souls is to undertake tasks for the betterment of the world. This will not just help them expand their own legacy of good deeds but will also be a major step in elevating their own consciousness.

2. **Inspiring positivity in others**

   Isn't it true that just by being in the presence of someone happy and positive, we feel energised and inspired? This happens because the energy of a happy soul has the power to influence us positively and create a powerful difference within us. Hence, the next mandate for happy souls is to connect ignorant minds with their own latent tendency to be happy. And they can do this either through their own shining example or by creating something that can help others discover their own inner happiness. This can include creations such as music, audio-visual entertainment, or even a book.

3. **Progressing spiritually**

   Only from a state of inner happiness can spiritual growth be sought and achieved. One cannot expect souls that are confused, struggling, or anxious to grasp life's deeper subjects. They first need to declutter their inner state. Also, another important criterion for progressing spiritually is contentment. This is because only when one is content can they think of something other than the mundane and thereby grasp the non-material aspects of life. And since this criterion is fulfilled by happy souls, they need to embark upon this journey of self-realisation. This will help them become aware of their own hidden potential and abilities and evolve as beings.

Also, as we have discussed earlier, inner progress becomes easier when one has less karmic debts. And we already know that the reason why happy souls can operate through a clear consciousness is because their debts have been settled in the past, making them perfect candidates for this karmic mandate.

Chapter 18

STRUGGLING SOULS

Struggle, in simple terms, means facing difficult circumstances over which one has little control. And in such a situation, the only way to survive is to endure. Therefore, for those who are struggling, life can become a long-drawn war which tests their willpower and inner strength.

But struggle, like any other aspect of life, isn't one-dimensional. It has its advantages even though the person struggling may find this hard to believe. The fact is that if one can endure and face whatever life throws their way with patience, fortitude, and resilience then they are sure to gain inner strength and courage, which makes up soul power. So, we can see that struggle is not all bad, and rather, it is a vital aspect of life as it helps us regain our lost powers and become more powerful as a being.

So, based on the definition above, we can say that struggling souls are souls who are caught in a constant battle of sorts. This battle would essentially be related to finances, and sometimes, these battles could revolve around relationships or health issues.

So, even though the type of struggle a soul undergoes may vary, they have to sacrifice a lot of their own self, their dreams, desires, interests, and most of all, their time. Crossing one hurdle after another, these souls have little choice but to endure the hardships and carry on despite the fatigue, which is bound to come with endless struggles. But even though one may think that life is being unfair to them, as mentioned earlier, there is a hidden purpose to their struggle that never quite allows them to quit. After all, it is for a reason that our life is mapped around a set of circumstances and one can make better sense of the same only by trying to understand the self, one's tendencies, and one's response to life. And it is the struggles of life that reveal a lot about one's strengths and weaknesses.

By now, we understand that we create the circumstances for the self which is based on our response to life in our previous forms. Thus, in the case of struggling souls, it is likely that their response to life in their previous lifetimes might have been a bit reckless. And a few primary reasons that could have landed them here include:

- Resistance to what is
- Lack of empathy
- Lack of commitment and loyalty
- Abuse of wealth and resources
- Lethargy or lack of hard work
- Excessive material conditioning
- Negligence or abuse of the body

Let us now understand how this works.

Resistance to life means living in denial and showing unwillingness to go with the flow of life. It also means we put too many question marks on tough situations or we try and ignore them for as long as we can, hoping for a miracle but don't do enough to successfully overcome them. So, for struggling souls, their past resistance is the key culprit for what they may be facing today as what one resists persists and gets even more challenging.

In case of relationship struggles, lack of empathy, not doing enough for others, and withholding love, respect, and acceptance may be seen as the main reason; besides loyalty and commitment issues.

In case of financial struggles, past patterns may include overspending, wastage of wealth and resources, greed, making money using unfair means, even tax evasion, or some level of unscrupulous behaviour that results in the disregard of liquid wealth. Also, excessive attachment to wealth due to heavy material conditioning creates fear around wealth and makes one a hoarder and miser. Another scenario would be having access to easy moncy and not working hard to multiply the same or recklessly spending it.

Lastly, a struggle in the present form regarding health (one's own or of anyone dependent) emerges from a lack of attention to physical well-being, fitness, and exercise. In certain serious cases, even abuse of the body through extreme habits and in worst-case scenarios, misuse of one's skills and knowledge to exploit people in the name of healthcare. These are the few reasons which can create a life path of struggle for a soul who may have in the past lived ignorantly or unconsciously.

The Karmic Mandates for Struggling Souls

These are the three essential present-life karmic mandates for struggling souls:

1. **Accepting what is**

   Any kind of struggle in life prevails till the time we don't accept it. The more we resist or try and reject the struggle, the stronger and longer it gets. Though once we accept the struggle, once we stop resisting it, we are at peace. We are no longer in denial of what is. In other words, we are no longer in desperation to change things. Desperation that depletes our inner powers and makes our energy heavy. But when we accept and are at peace, we shift our own energy to a positive vibration. And from there, we attract better opportunities and life experiences.

Therefore, the first important mandate for struggling souls is to not reject what is. Because if we reject struggles that come our way, we are bound to lose peace and power and as a result, struggle more. Here, it is important to understand that when the focus is to resist the struggle or have any kind of negative emotion towards it, one is only giving more power to the struggle. Hence, our struggles double, because now, they become both internal and external which makes it all the more difficult to change things. But when one accepts and goes with life, one creates the opposite energy in which struggle cannot find continuity.

2. **Embracing humility**

As we have seen earlier, struggling souls have made certain mistakes in the past due to which they have to face struggles in life but these struggles are full of lessons. Therefore, when a soul goes through the grind, it must not consider itself less fortunate. For it has simply chosen a tougher way to learn its lessons and the physical and material hardships are only meant to soften the soul deep within and help break the ego. This means that the mandate for struggling souls is to embrace the opposite of the ego, which is humility. Humility is necessary to help these souls value their health, wealth, and relationships. As only when one is humble can they understand that they are capable of mistakes and this realisation allows one to change things. Otherwise, one continues living in denial and resisting life.

Therefore, struggling souls need to remember that their present life, which may feel like a rude awakening, is meant to instil greater humility and direct their consciousness towards learning from their struggles. And learning is also the only way to make their struggles well worth it!

3. **Living with empathy, commitment, and compassion**

When it comes to relationship struggles, they are meant to make these souls humble and teach them how to live with cooperation and compassion and not indifference and ego, which creates unhappy relationships. Thus, an important mandate for these souls is to value others more, understand them at a deeper level, and feel empathy despite any differences in personalities. This would allow them to rise above their own limited self and understand what it takes to give and support others.

Their karmic mandate is to learn the art of cooperation, adjustment, and respect for other people's perspectives and give their love, care, and loyalty without holding back or without expecting the same in return. Expecting the same would prove counterproductive as it would make things conditional from their end. Something that hinders healthy relationships.

These souls also need to remain aware of their karmic debts which need to be settled. So, they may face resistance from the other side, which acts as a block. And this is because in the past there were mistakes made from their end, which perhaps caused emotional strife in others. So now, these souls may have to handle added pressure in their relationships and the resistance they could be facing is the return of past karma, which they need to settle with patience, acceptance, and empathy.

Chapter 19
LOST SOULS

Some souls are bored with life and one can see this boredom manifest in their approach and attitude towards life. Thus, one can find them going about life in a very passive manner and doing the same things day after day and living in constant monotony. Although jaded, these souls neither have the inclination nor the mindset to come out of their repetitive pattern and experiment with new and unfamiliar things. Not only do such souls lack excitement and the will to experiment and seek new ideas, but they also dislike change. Thus, they lead a fixed and fairly lacklustre existence. And these uninspired and unimaginative souls can be termed lost souls.

Given the extreme monotony and the tedious, one-dimensional nature of their lives, lost souls often get confused as lazy or stubborn but in reality, they are neither. They are simply those who prefer to remain indifferent to the more exciting and experimental side of life because they don't believe it can offer anything new or anything that would be different from what they already have. It is for this reason they resist participating wholeheartedly in life and avoid doing what is required of them. Even though such souls may have a reasonably full life externally, yet, mentally and psychologically, they remain dull, subdued, and a bit clueless. What they lack most is the spark of creativity, the keenness to explore life, the drive to do more than what's necessary, and the curiosity and love for life. One will rarely find these souls embarking upon an adventure or engaging with something unfamiliar or taking risks, as they just do not have the thrill of seeking. Fairly conventional, these souls stay confined to societal norms or their own mind-made boundaries. And so, they simply exist and rarely live their life the way it must be lived.

One will find such souls doing only as much is necessary for survival and need. Not to say this is wrong, but sadly, these souls don't get to experience life at its fullest. Perhaps, their exposure to life has always been limited and they cannot fathom the immense possibilities that could be explored. Perhaps, they don't understand the prospects that life holds and all that can be achieved beyond the necessary. Or perhaps they haven't been challenged enough by life and experiences to seek something more. So, they have no particular goal, motivation, aspiration, drive, purpose, or even ambition. And it is precisely for this reason they come across as aimless and lost.

Their unhealthy mental blocks are a stark contrast to a world that's constantly seeking and striving for newer experiences. And these blocks not only weigh them down but also push them towards more boredom and cluelessness. The same gets harder because this restriction of the mind is self-imposed due to one's own inability to see things differently.

Lost souls can be some of the kindest and nicest souls around. It is just that it is hard for them to appreciate the self and the things around them due to their limited take on life and restricted reference points. It also might seem that these souls fear leaving the security and comfort of a routine and are afraid of taking risks, or that they are pessimistic, but the fact is that they are simply not interested in the exploration and discovery of something new, enriching, enigmatic, or something far more stimulating as they believe that it does not exist.

So, we can see that the key factors responsible for the repetitive nature of their lives include:

- Lack of perspective
- Zero curiosity towards life
- Lack of exposure to new things
- Lack of challenges
- Excessive identification with the mind
- Lack of self-awareness

And if we delve deeper into the cause of their nature, we will find that their boredom or cluelessness emerges from a very limited context of life. This could be because their past lives were one-dimensional and didn't challenge them enough to seek new avenues or redefine their life. It is also possible that in their past lives, these souls were so consumed with honouring their fixed set of material or worldly duties that they were unable to expand their mental horizon or embrace a more elevated and creative context of life. Another possibility is that they have undergone several lifetimes in which they were restricted to just the mundane material activities. Like doing a routine job and not seeking anything beyond it due to material compulsions or fear. Or being in a business that was passed on to them as an inheritance. It is also likely that some of these souls had a very confined life as they had to take care of family duties, traditions, legacy, etc. Perhaps, they were exposed to only the material side of life—duties, responsibilities, liabilities, and pressures of keeping things going. And so, they remained unexposed to the creative, mystical, spiritual, adventurous, and enjoyable aspects of life. It is likely that these souls didn't get a chance to understand what they were capable of doing or explore something other than what was mandated by society or their immediate environment. For example, in certain families, the children are expected to continue what their forefathers did and denied a chance to explore and understand their own individual dreams and potential. Another example could be when women are expected to look after their families and live in a routine that tramples their own hidden potential. And if one constantly attaches greater importance to other people's needs and ignores their own, a sense of dullness, cluelessness, and boredom is bound to prevail, which is the real problem with lost souls. They are habitually indisposed to change. Additionally, their lack of exposure to a multi-layered and multi-dimensional existence in the past has made them lose a deeper connection with the self. Due to this, they've remained completely detached from the grander prospects or the sweeter and subtler flow of life, which is essential to nourish one's spirit and open the mind to various possibilities and interests.

With a limited filter to see the world, these souls, in their past, became so consumed in their fixed material chase that they lost a wider interest in life. Their blinkered approach prevented them from tapping into a larger part of their potential and reduced most of their creative and imaginative faculties. This, in turn, may have contributed to the loss of their inner liveliness. After all, a one-dimensional existence can be all-exhausting and offers nothing that rejuvenates and inspires the spirit, which mostly seeks the opposite and flourishes in the more multi-dimensional, creative, and challenging aspects of life.

The Karmic Mandates for Lost Souls

The three essential present-life karmic mandates for lost souls include:

1. **Reinvent the self**

   An important thing for lost souls is to focus inwards and take out time for self-nourishment as they need a lot of inner work. They need to awaken to their true self and unlock their own hidden potential. This is their first karmic mandate. And for this, they need to prioritise themselves. They need to become conscious of their strengths and weaknesses and work on living with greater self-awareness.

   To bring about any significant change in themselves, these souls need to first identify, accept, and deal with their real cause of feeling lost and uninspired, which ostensibly comes from their own limited understanding of life. So, they need to expand their awareness of not just the world outside but also their own inner world. As until this full-fledged awareness blossoms, they may not be able to bring about any positive change.

   In order to generate this awareness, lost souls need to observe life and fully engage with it. They must also break the monotony of their worldly pursuits and go towards things that help them get out of their shell. And once they become self-aware, these souls need to take the necessary steps to reinvent the self, which amounts to:

   - Choosing to grow
   - Embracing new ideas

- Building inner resources
- Being broad-minded
- Being multifaceted
- Having long-term and short-term goals
- Actively seeking something more in terms of knowledge and experience
- Not being aimless or powerless
- Feeling driven and inspired
- Becoming smarter and wiser

2. **Challenge the self**

The second karmic mandate for lost souls is to evolve by challenging the self and gaining perspective. As unless these souls challenge the self adequately, they won't be able to break the inertia or the conditioning that has long set in. They will also not be able to discover their true potential and their latent talents, gifts, and capabilities.

So, in order to achieve their mandate, these souls need to increase their participation in life and do things which they instinctively feel they have never done before. Or things that even make them uncomfortable because they certainly need to be more experimental and push themselves harder towards doing things that are not within their comfort. Challenging the self is a definite pending karma for these souls as it is something they've not been able to do before. So, most likely, their present life will either bring them to a point where challenges would become inevitable and where these souls will feel compelled to break their long reconciliation with the ordinariness of life.

Most of their challenges would amount to doing a bit more than what's needed, thinking differently, responding fearlessly, stepping out of old patterns, experimenting with a multi-dimensional life, and leading a life that is a stark contrast to how they've lived before and one that has many kinds of exposures and interactions that help these souls expand their world view.

3. **Being multidimensional**

As discussed, lost souls have missed the real context of life and have invested themselves heavily in things that could not help them evolve as a soul. Therefore, their present mandate is to redefine their very context of life. And the only way they can do so is by broadening their horizon.

In other words, they need to take steps to be multi-dimensional. This includes being more creative, experimental, research-driven, and adventurous and engaging in activities such as reading, writing, painting, sculpting, photography, designing, dancing, singing, playing musical instruments, performing arts, gardening, cooking, and learning new languages. They can also participate in some sort of group activities or sports such as yoga, swimming, mountaineering etc., or simply spend time in nature. Travel also is a must for them along with exposure to different cultures and ways of life. All such activities can be therapeutic for them and can expose them to new and interesting ideas that will help them expand their vision of the world and life in general. Such activities will also help release them from their mind-made prison and break the monotony of their outlook. They will also help create new desires and find a new purpose and meaning in life as well as rediscover lost enthusiasm.

Another thing that will help lost souls honour their karmic mandate is making the effort to understand the non-material side of life and pursue something that charges their inner aliveness and helps bring some music to their soul! Things like poetry, history, philosophy, and spiritual and mystical studies are great options as they will not just help them address their inner vacuum but also radically improve their perspective of life.

Chapter 20

UNSUCCESSFUL SOULS

The definition of success varies for each one of us. There are people who without any significant achievements feel successful, while some enjoy the journey to their goals and find that satisfying, and then there are people who despite a great number of achievements feel unsuccessful. The truth is that success has no universal barometer and similar to peace, happiness, and gratitude, it is an inner thing.

And as the name entails, unsuccessful souls are those who do not feel successful. They may be achievers in the worldly sense but in their own eyes, they remain unsuccessful. Such souls constantly strive for more and are ever in pursuit of something that exceeds their own imagination. And even if they are able to get what they desire, their quest for more never ends.

These souls spend their entire life pursuing their ambitions, desires, and goals. One can even call them dissatisfied souls, but their dissatisfaction leads them to something more damaging and regrettable and it's the feeling of being unsuccessful. Though it's not that these souls are plain greedy or over-ambitious, they simply aren't able to access the satisfaction that must come with achievement and the gratitude that must follow. And because they remain thankless, unsuccessful souls are neither able to enjoy whatever little or big success that comes their way nor are they able to celebrate life and their journey. Thus, the feeling of being unsuccessful remains.

On closer observation, we can see that the main issue lies in the fact that these souls don't quite acknowledge what they have and rather, they just acknowledge the feeling of deficiency. Something inside these souls keeps telling them that their success can get better, that it's not enough, and there is more to be achieved. And this pattern doesn't arise from overconfidence or some sort of narcissism. Instead, it arises from the vacuum within them and the desperation to fill it anyhow.

This habit of never pausing and always chasing the next goal makes them emotionally cluttered and anxious. Not only that, but they also lose track of the self due to this never-ending hustle. Hence, they remain disconnected from what they have or where they are and invest their energy on where they could be. In short, they are constantly driven by their desire for the next big thing. This could be the next big opportunity, promotion, rank, etc., or a bigger pay cheque, a bigger assignment, a bigger project, bigger acquisitions, bigger mergers, bigger targets, bigger profits, bigger assets, etc. This can also include more reputation, status, fame, or even better relationships and fancier assets, bigger social engagements, bigger indulgences, or even better life situations.

Thus, an entire life is spent chasing something, pushing the self harder each day, working tirelessly, and doing things beyond one's capacity in order to feel bigger, better, and more successful than others. And yet, the feeling of success continues to elude these souls because they don't give themselves a chance to merge with it or spend time enjoying it. Basically, they don't stop and cherish all the creations of success—rest, comfort, enjoyment, celebrations, family, travel, or even just some alone time that leads to the rejuvenation of one's spirit.

Though their preference to chase goals over catching sunsets qualifies them as hard workers, it doesn't always make them a star performer or a winner. Because for one to perform to the best of their ability, there must be peace within. And peace is what eludes workaholics which is also the reason why they push themselves beyond a limit that's normal. And because these souls remain peaceless, they are neither able to process their intentions correctly nor execute their actions effectively. The same leads to more dissatisfaction in them and a bigger ego. The fact is that when we aren't grateful, our energy gets heavier due to a lack of positive emotions and the constant pressure for more. And the same leads to more anxiety, thanklessness, and chaos within, which further feed the ego.

And so, the irony is that once these souls achieve their desired goals, they lose interest in the same. Soon, they move their focus to their next set of goals and by doing so, not only do they dishonour their efforts but also deny the self an opportunity to feel grateful and fulfilled, which, in turn, continues to inflate their ego.

From a closer observation, it becomes evident that the past lives of these souls have been quite hard on them. It is likely that there may have been a lot of competition, comparison, and even criticism that they had to endure in their previous lifetimes. It is also possible that they may have also been non-achievers in the worldly sense. Meaning, that they couldn't achieve much in terms of rank, power, social status, wealth, or any other material achievement. And the only way these souls learnt to assess themselves is through the yardstick of material success. Perhaps, they had demanding parents or a spouse, who expected a lot from them and subjected these souls to extreme forms of mental harassment and pressure.

Also, the ego is the enemy here because not only does it condition the mind to operate out of fear and a definite lack, but somewhere it also gives rise to low self-esteem. And this low self-esteem drives these souls towards a constant pursuit.

And what is the ego? It is a false sense of the self. It is our conditioning of the mind due to past experiences and the wrong reference points, which constantly tell us that we aren't enough. The ego is what makes us feel deficient, inferior, and insecure. It makes us hanker for more because it makes us think quite poorly of the self. And so, it creates fear. This includes fear of failure, lack, inadequacy, and most importantly, fear of criticism and rejection and fear of losing something personally and socially.

Ego also reduces us to a bundle of doubts and from these doubts arises the feeling of not having enough. It makes us seek power and control in order to feel complete, but this completion never comes and we end up seeking endlessly. Ego also makes a lot of noise and keeps the mind busy and confused. This way, it neither allows us to listen to our conscience nor does it let the intellect intervene. It also holds on to past wounds and they continue to persist as feelings of self-doubt and self-pity. Hence, it doesn't allow healing and change. So regardless of the change in our external situations, if there's ego, one doesn't get detached from feelings of past hurt or emotional abuse.

An important point to note here is that since there's very little talk about ego, one hardly understands its evils. And so, unsuccessful souls rarely get the knowledge or an environment where they can heal through understanding and self-awareness. And since they lack self-awareness, they always remain in a quest to satisfy their ego. With time, their ego keeps getting bigger, stronger, and more menacing. Because a strong ego only keeps them trapped in worldly pursuits and the material chase and hence, there is no room for their inner awakening, healing, and growth.

So, this category of souls needs to reclaim their true powers and for that, they must work on the ego. Because as long as they remain unaware and live out of ignorance, their lives will remain an excruciating journey of self-torture and persistent self-doubt.

The Karmic Mandates for Unsuccessful Souls

These are the three essential present life karmic mandates for unsuccessful souls:

1. **Dissolving ego**

   There is no magic formula for dissolving the ego. It involves a tremendous amount of hard work and self-awareness. And these souls need to put in this hard work in order to reclaim their inner powers. Meaning, they need to first and foremost understand what the ego is and its presence in them. They can learn this through the right wisdom on the subject or by seeking help as they definitely need a guide in their lives. This can include a mentor, life coach, spiritual teacher, or even a psychologist who can unravel before them, their true state of consciousness and the influence of ego.

   Some of the crucial steps involved in dissolving the ego are as follows:

   - Understanding what exactly ego is and how it operates in our psyche. This understanding must also lead to a conscious realisation of having an ego. Otherwise, nothing really can be done to dissolve it. And often, it is the ego that becomes the barrier when it comes to accepting this fact.

- Balancing our outer and inner life is the next most important thing. Being focused on the outer life inflates the ego, as then, the ego remains unchecked. Therefore, paying attention to one's inner life, one's inner self, helps identify the ego and fix it.
- Stepping out of our ignorance and unconscious patterns of behaviour and living consciously while learning to dissolve all egoic patterns through the application of higher wisdom and self-awareness.
- Not clinging to the conditioned mind-made image of the self or relying on others in order to make one feel important or special. Cultivating a healthy self-image which is not dependent on any external factors especially, the praise and criticism of others, is very important.
- Changing our perspective and challenging our conditioning. This involves letting go of old thoughts and beliefs and boosting our daily intake of positive information, conversations, and affirmations. Another important step is to experiment with new and empowering ideas and adopt these as a way of life.

2. Healing

The next important karmic mandate for these souls is to heal. Due to their long-standing ego, these souls grapple with a sense of emptiness. It happens because the ego drains out our spiritual powers as it makes us operate through undesirable tendencies such as fear, anger, insecurity, etc. This can cause mental fatigue and the only way to revive oneself is through healing.

Healing happens when one broadens their horizon and engages in the complete experience of life. Meaning, one leads a balanced life which entails giving equal attention to all important aspects such as personal life, work, fitness, recreation, spending time with the self, being in nature, practising stillness, engaging in some form of higher learning and wisdom, etc.

Professional counselling is another good option to heal the ever-persistent stress. It can make them understand and eliminate their hidden fears and their nagging sense of self-doubt. Basically, anything that helps release their emotional toxins can be very useful because ego tends to create a lot of unnecessary emotional baggage. Therefore, seeking a professional counsellor, a guide, or a spiritual teacher can help these souls feel relaxed and this relaxation can help build a positive environment within them, which is very important to break the ego.

Stepping away from the noise of their mind and being in stillness from time to time, as well as imbibing spiritual wisdom are also powerful steps that will help with healing and if one can do so daily, it can alter the way one thinks and help connect with their higher self. Stillness helps break the momentum of unhealthy thinking patterns and creates space between thoughts that is necessary for the mind to embrace new and creative thoughts which help break the conditioning of the ego.

3. **Accepting what is**

An essential mandate for souls who feel they are unsuccessful is to become present. And this means remaining fully attentive to what is in their life and feeling one with the present moment. So, not only do their thoughts need to be around what is, but they also need to fully feel whatever the present has to offer. This can help enhance their self-image because this way, these souls will be able to connect emotionally with their achievements and experience them to the fullest as and when they happen. This will also help them stay grateful, which is essential to boost self-esteem and creating a feeling of well-being.

Being present and accepting what is also ensures that there is no resistance to life. So, regardless of what life brings, if these souls learn to accept everything that comes their way and experience it wholeheartedly, they'll be able to drop all forms of resistance. And by dropping resistance, they'll drop the ego. Because ego likes to cling to things and especially things of the past. But it can't survive in the now. Therefore, living life in the now is the easiest way to destroy the ego.

Chapter 21
REJECTED SOULS

Rejection can come to a soul from any front and at any point in time. However, there are some souls who encounter rejection far too many times in their life for various reasons. These souls remain perplexed about why things turn against them so often. The repeated pattern of rejection in their lives can be baffling and because there are times when it happens for a reason that's too trivial or hard to understand and accept, it leaves these souls demoralised.

Some of the different forms of rejection that these souls face include:

- Rejection which comes unexpectedly.
- Rejection in the workspace which can be either in form of rejection of one's ideas or projects or being denied a job or promotion which might be overdue.
- Rejection in marital relationship, i.e., their partner may not remain inclined to continue.
- Rejection in matters of the heart, i.e., their love may stay unrequited.
- Rejection in the family, i.e., their sibling may get more love and attention.
- Rejection from the extended family.

- Other forms of rejections like their loan application being rejected or their visa not getting approved.
- Rejection in getting a university admission and other academic pursuits.
- Rejection from society, i.e., some sort of victory or honour and appreciation can elude them.

Likewise, there can be many other forms of rejection. And these rejections can happen consistently for one or more reasons, leaving these souls heartbroken. And since we have never really been taught how to interpret or handle rejection in life, it can lead to a lot of shame and self-pity. Such emotions can damage the psyche and cause harm beyond what one can imagine.

And this happens because rejection has been always seen as a negative experience. Primarily because the human mind has been trained to see approval and acceptance as necessary and when the opposite happens, our conditioning tells us that something terrible has happened or that one is unworthy of good things. And it is again ego that makes us see rejection as something unfortunate and as something that reflects poorly on us. But why is it so? To understand this we need to realise that rejection, like all other human experiences, is an integral part of human life and that it happens for a reason.

The truth about rejection is that souls facing the same too often may just have a lot to learn about the self and about the subtler ways, in which life operates.

As mentioned, there is no doubt that rejection can be difficult to comprehend, especially, parental rejection or being rejected at a very young age which can create a lasting impact on our psyche. And the hurt of rejection gets amplified further when we do not understand why we are constantly being rejected. Or when we subscribe to the popular view that rejection is demeaning and it must evoke disappointment and pity. But then, behind every rejection, there is always a reason, and that reason is something, which we all need to familiarise ourselves with, in order to go past any sort of hurt and even break this chain of rejections.

So, let us understand why some souls have to endure a greater number of rejections than others.

1. Energy

Rejections can happen at any age or stage of life. But the main cause of rejection is one's own energy. As we have already covered in the previous chapters, energy is the most important aspect of a soul as it shapes every soul's destiny. Energy is the quality or the state of the soul and it is this energy which determines the quality of the soul's experiences. And what is it that gives this energy its quality or character? It is a soul's thoughts, emotions, feelings, behaviour, and all that a soul carries in its memory. On this depends the quality of a soul's experiences in life. Also, each soul is unique owing to its unique energy and it attracts experiences similar to its energy.

So, when a soul carries some sort of hurt, pain, or self-doubt as its deepest emotions, its energy becomes somewhat dark, complex, and heavy. And this energy is bound to attract experiences equally complex and heavy, which includes rejection as well. And the longer a soul sustains this energy, the longer the pattern of rejection or any sort of negative experience will exist. This pattern could also be repetitive because, with every rejection, the soul is likely to create more negativity and hurt.

Thus, one can continue getting hurt repeatedly without understanding that it is their own energy which is attracting the hurt-inducing experience in their life. The other alternative is that we can leave our hurt of the past and renew the self with faith, self-confidence, self-love, and self-belief and create positive energy, leading to better and happier experiences. Therefore, how we look, talk, and act matters little as all these aspects only have a superficial impact. In fact, it is our energy which creates a deeper and long-lasting impact.

Therefore, rejection has a lot to do with the way we feel and what we think all the time. So, if our subconscious has patterns of poor self-image, constant self-doubt, or even tendencies of self-rejection, or if we question the self too often and carry emotional wounds or negative impressions, then this will result in an accumulation of negative energy which, in turn, will adversely affect people's perceptions and feelings about us. The big irony about rejection is that we unknowingly ask for it and then suffer!

Also, because we all are eternal beings who keep on taking a new life one after another, our energy remains with us through all these lives. In fact, the only thing that gets transferred with the soul from one life to another is its energy.

So, we can see that even in the case of a small child, the accumulated energy of past lives, which reaches others as the vibration of his or her soul, is the key to what others feel or think about the child. And this includes the parents! Therefore, the more complex or heavier the energy, the greater the chances of the child being discriminated against.

In the given context, one needs to understand that a child is only a child in the physical sense but as a being or a soul, the child is actually ageless! And it is this soul, which carries a certain quality of energy from the past that becomes the key to deciding its present life experiences.

Thus, it becomes of vital importance to analyse and improve our energy with every lifetime in order to free the self from any kind of negativity and create positive emotions and experiences.

2. Past energy exchanges

Another reason why rejections happen is because of a soul's familiarity with it. This means that the soul has invested energy in rejecting others in the past. Call it out of ignorance, arrogance, or lack of empathy, rejected souls have exchanged energy with other souls in their past lives, using rejection in their thoughts, feelings, and actions. And so now, rejection isn't just a part of their karmic burden, it is also something they need to experience and change.

Thus, we can see that rejection has its roots in our past lives or in the energy we carry from past lives. And given the way the law of karma operates, it makes it mandatory for one to experience the same energy that was once released by them in the form of intentions, thoughts, words, feelings, and actions. This can either be good or bad energy. But only when this energy returns to its original essence, the karma between the giver and the receiver moves towards settlement. So, the energy of rejection returns as an experience of rejection for the one who may have ignorantly, carelessly, or callously rejected others in the past. Therefore, unless there is a solid ground to reject someone (it is justified) and there is a conscious use of rejection (it is expressed with compassion for the other), particularly in close relationships, karmic debts build up. And it is such debts that attract the energy of rejection in one's life. And this is the subtler truth about rejections that one needs to be aware of.

The Karmic Mandates for Rejected Souls

The three essential present-life karmic mandates for rejected souls include:

1. **Have more acceptance**

   Building acceptance is a major karmic mandate for these souls. This is not just about accepting people as they are but also all situations and life experiences. So, say if these souls meet any kind of rejection in their life, they need to accept this rejection and not try to resist it in any manner. This is important because acceptance creates peace and resistance builds negative emotions such as fear, anger, and hurt as well as leads to a victim mentality. So, when we resist our life situations, we punish ourselves and become bitter. Such bitterness combined with our negative emotions makes our energy negative and incapable of attracting things that are positive. In such a scenario, we are likely to face more rejection in life.

   Whereas when we accept life situations, which may even involve rejection, it no longer remains rejection as it transforms into acceptance. This acceptance is a positive response and it creates peace within us and further attracts experiences that are positive in nature. In fact, most of our life problems prevail when we show resistance to them. Therefore, we must learn to create the opposite energy in problematic situations as that's how we will be able to save ourselves from suffering and from drawing more problems in our life. Also, when we accept something like rejection without any judgement or resistance, we show humility. This humility is penance. For should we have made any mistakes in the past, mistakes of rejecting irresponsibly, our mind must remain open to understanding and acknowledging the same. And this demands humility which, in the given situation, amounts to penance.

2. **Understand rejection**

Rejection may be labelled as something disappointing, but it is actually an experience of life that is connected to an energy exchange in the past where one may have been responsible for rejecting others. Past here infers to past lives, where one may have engaged in senseless rejection of others. But rejection as we know is a part of life that cannot be totally eliminated. So, as long as humans interact and are exchanging energies through deeds, emotions, thoughts, and feelings or even in the mundane activities of life, rejection is going to be a part of one's journey.

What's important is to not take this rejection to the heart and create negative emotions around it. This way, the energy of rejection doesn't rub on the soul and it remains light and unaffected. Therefore, as a part of their karmic mandate, rejected souls must learn to not absorb the opinions of others, especially the negative ones, and convert them into deep feelings. By acknowledging rejection through their thoughts and by feeling rejected or demoralised, these souls complicate their own energy and give permanence to rejections in their life.

The truth is when we don't think of rejection as rejection and accept it as an experience of life, it becomes powerless and ineffective. But if the same thing is held for too long in one's emotional memory, its intensity and hold on us increases.

Also, all rejections must be respected as someone's choice or free will and not a way to assess one's own value in life as this can be exceedingly damaging, unhealthy, and unnecessary. One needs to understand that rejection of any sort is an external event, dependent on external factors, which they have no control over. Therefore, the experience of rejection must never be taken personally and shouldn't be seen as a threshold to evaluate one's own worth and importance. This is an important lesson that rejected souls need to understand in order to release negative emotions and break the continued pattern of rejection in their life.

To conclude, we need to understand that rejection, like any other experience of life, comes to change us for the better and teach us some valuable lessons that can help us progress to a more mature and evolved state of being. One could also say that rejection is, yet another means to help us stay strong and less complacent. So, instead of getting bogged down or feeling hurt, victimised, or angry by any kind of rejection, we need to change our outlook and see rejection as an opportunity to check and change the self for the better. And it is by being more encouraging, patient, and kind towards the self, we make rejection an instrument of positive transformation.

3. Loving the self

Rejected souls tend to undervalue themselves because their love for the self is conditional. It is based on their external experiences and so, these souls are deficient in self-love. Self-love is definitely a karmic mandate that these souls need to honour.

Self-love means unconditionally accepting, loving, and appreciating the self and not relying on life experiences and other people to make one feel good about the self. In other words, self-love means having high self-worth. This involves engaging in positive self-talk and respecting the self at all times, despite any rejections in life.

Rejected souls need to remember that self-respect is nurtured when we understand and accept our flaws or imperfections and work on them rather than feel miserable about them or criticise the self for the same. The important thing that such souls need to bear in mind is that people reject their energy; they do not reject them! And people reject their energy because it is heavy and somewhat dark which makes them uncomfortable and uneasy. Therefore, all that rejected souls need to do is change the quality of their energy with the help of self-introspection, motivation, and constant self-encouragement.

Chapter 22

COMPETITIVE SOULS

Competition is good as long as it doesn't become an obsession. An obsession to overtake others and feel superior as a result or to fill one's own void, which is a creation of the ego. So, while being competitive in today's times may be a common thing, there are some souls who are born competitive. These souls show an unhealthy competitive streak and an insatiable desire to stay ahead of others at a very young age. This is because they have an uncontrollable zeal to prove something in life and remain keen to outdo their rivals, regardless of their own capability and means. They also do not take kindly to failure or any kind of restraint while competing. And when they are engaged in a race with someone, even the smallest of disappointments tend to affect them a great deal. Also, in such a scenario, they can be harsh on themselves. In short, their whole life seems mapped around being competitive as these souls actually seek competition the most. In fact, their competitive spirit can rise at the slightest provocation.

If we talk about their outlook, competitive souls tend to see life as a race, where their main aim is to always stay ahead of those who they consider as competition. And pushed by this constant urge, they can even come off as being aggressive and ruthless. These souls are always ready to challenge others and sometimes, they even compete just for the thrill of it. In fact, more than the accolades and success, they live to prove a point to others. They are keen to shine and believe that being in some sort of competition is the only way to achieve it. It gives them a feeling that they are something, some sort of an achiever and more competent. So, be it in academics or professional life or in any other field or activity, these souls want to excel through competition. It makes them feel good about the self and adds more meaning and value to their self-image. And this isn't because they have low self-esteem but because they are on a mission to prove something.

There are also times when these souls may not seem to be visibly competing with others, but in their heads, they are always calculating their own strengths and weaknesses versus that of those who are in their realm of work or those with who they may be competing against. Therefore, even when they do not seem to be competing directly, the competitive spirit of these souls keeps ticking all the time.

Also, participating in some form of competition, direct or indirect, can be very reassuring for them as only when they have someone to compare or compete with, they feel they can assess the self better. And though their individual achievements could be enough to satisfy them, until these souls find the self ahead of others against whom they might be psychologically or physically competing, they do not feel triumphant or gratified.

Another feature of competitive souls is that age is not a barrier for them and the limitations of life or circumstances matter little when it comes to achieving a goal through competition. Basically, once they set their eyes on a rival, then nothing can come in their way. They need to compete and win, regardless of the end gain. So, what they are chasing doesn't matter as much as outdoing their competition. And every time they succeed in beating their opponent, it further fuels their fire towards competition in life. In fact, it is this unquenchable desire that keeps them motivated and satisfied as their thrill is not in achieving something but in competing and beating an opponent.

It can be said that competitive souls relentlessly pursue competition for their own sake. There is no other reason why these souls cannot stop throwing the self into some form of challenge. They also do not compete in phases and are not picky or moody about when or with whom they want to compete. So, one can find them competing at home, in their workplace, in their social circles . . . basically, just about everywhere they are involved. And they could compete for even the smallest, the most insignificant things as it is the competition that satisfies their inner hunger and makes them feel energised.

But due to this constant urge to prove themselves, these souls can at times be too harsh on themselves. This arises because they always have this restless energy, nervousness, and an ego-driven attachment to prove a point. They simply want to stay ahead of those who they consider their direct competition. So, you'll find these souls competing with siblings, co-workers, their close friends, and just about anyone who triggers their competitive urge. They, in fact, don't choose their rivals but instead choose to simply compete and create rivals in order to be engaged in some form of competition. And their spirit of competition may not necessarily be always healthy. Many times, it can involve jealousy that could start it all and lead them into fierce competition with anyone who triggers their deep-rooted insecurities.

So, let us inspect what makes competitive souls who they are. Given their insecure nature and their desperation to compete, these souls, in their past lives, were likely deprived of opportunities to prove themselves and enjoy the success they may have rightfully deserved. It also could be that in their past lives, these souls were treated unfairly or were denied the freedom to explore their calibre. It is also possible that they were discriminated against or they watched others from the sidelines, those less capable, enjoying better freedom, opportunities, and success. Perhaps, these souls had to live in other people's shadows or put others before the self every time. Perhaps, they stayed repressed due to some kind of external pressure or domination, which hardly allowed them to stand up for themselves, their rights, and their deepest wishes. Whatever the reason might have been, these souls probably had to make too many compromises in their previous lifetimes and sacrifice their own desires as a result. And due to this reason, their vast potential could not be realised.

Their aggression, which sparks the fire of competition in these souls, may actually be hidden anger that's rooted in feelings of deprivation and denial of their rights. Anger which is insurmountable and veiled and makes them hunt opponents from various walks of life. And it is this anger which contributes to making them headstrong about proving that they are better than others.

Quite evidently, these souls want to make up for their wasted past lives and so, they keep the self constantly engaged in some form of competition. Doing so not only excites them but also gives them a sense of complete involvement, freedom, and absolute participation in life. Something that was once denied to them and led to feelings of suppression. And it is this suppression that has now exploded into an unhealthy competitive streak. This prevents them from creating loving connections with others, in order to overcome the sense of being the outsider or the one who was wronged.

The Karmic Mandates for Competitive Souls

The three essential present-life karmic mandates for competitive souls include:

1. **Participate and not compete**

   An important karmic mandate to fulfil for competitive souls is to understand and enjoy the spirit of participation rather than competition. Just because there is a deep-rooted feeling of deprivation in them, they need not become vindictive. They need to realise that a competitive state of mind at all times is a sign of hidden anger and revenge and by being in constant competition, they aren't getting rid of their emotional baggage. Rather, they are further fueling their anger and aggression, which is harmful. This is yet another way of helping their ego grow as their sense of satisfaction, which comes through being superior to someone else, is a perfect environment for the ego.

   These souls need to understand that the thing they lack in their experience is wholehearted participation in life. This makes them engage in mindless competition with others and by doing so, they feel that they are reclaiming their power and authority in life, which is only a delusional way of understanding their own growth. Therefore, what these souls need is to expand their experience of life. The more they participate in all aspects of life, the more experience they will gain and the more enthusiasm and peace they will find. And the more peaceful these souls become, the more powerful and fulfilling will be their overall understanding of life. In short, their pride and joy should be rooted in peace as peace is a healthier way to feel complete and satisfied.

In whichever area these souls feel compelled to compete, what they need to do is simply give their best and not operate through the mindset or the pressure of competing. Because pressure and competition, both generate negative energy and this energy becomes a roadblock to achieving what these souls want in their life. This also pushes them to compete and remain in a never-ending search for competition. So, these souls need to shift focus from competition to expanding and enjoying their whole experience of life.

2. Make peace

Competitive souls need to make peace with themselves as this will help them drop their over-competitive side. But how can this peace be achieved?

The sense of deprivation in competitive souls manifests as jealousy in their relationships. And this jealousy gets more intense when it is honed by constant competitiveness. At times, the same jealousy when it leads to loss and defeat in life can make them more insecure and angrier, which further strengthens their ego and makes them indulge in more unhealthy competition. And this way, these souls remain in a loop.

Hence, it is imperative that they entirely focus on themselves and participate in life by being attentive to the self. This attention will not only help them understand how unfairly they have been treating the self but will also make them calmer and more effective in whatever they are doing. After all, when the focus is on an opponent, one's energy and effort both remain divided. But when the focus is on the self, then one becomes capable of drawing the best out of the self and their entire energy goes in the positive direction. Therefore, these souls need to pursue life with a single-minded focus as this will ensure that all kinds of pressure and turbulence remain at bay and also prevent jealous behaviour.

Peace for these souls can also be attained by letting go of harsh judgements of others which always arise from jealousy. When one analyses others or sees others as obstacles to their goals or their happiness, or when one continues to feel deprived, jealousy is imminent. Therefore, competitive souls need to make peace with others and develop a healthy outlook towards people in their lives.

Thus, the mandate for these souls is to break out from their cold and aloof self and be one with others. A healthy camaraderie and mixing up with other people will not only create more peace in these souls but also help them excel and do much more in life.

In a nutshell, being nonjudgmental, not giving more energy to critical feelings, practising forgiveness, and letting go of damaging emotions are some of the things they need to practice. And finally, if they can direct their mind to the lighter side of life, that can also help create inner peace.

3. Be effective and exciting

Instead of wasting energy in competing and in all the mental calculations needed to overcome competition, these souls need to preserve energy and utilise the same to be more effective in their area of activity or work. This will not just help them become the best version of themselves but will also get them the sort of response they seek from life and others.

So, we can say that an important mandate for competitive souls is to seek the maximum thrill in life and immerse the self in the joy of wholehearted participation. This will allow them to challenge the self and get more out of the self, which will automatically create satisfaction and enhanced self-worth. It will help them see the pointlessness of wasting energy in competing with others and will create a more positive life experience.

As mentioned earlier, competitive souls definitely have deep psychological baggage to deal with. But they need to remember that this baggage cannot be removed unless they create a more exciting and fulfilling life. A kind of life where they are involved completely and positively. This is something that can never happen through competition because competition never allows one to fully engage with life and also builds negative energy in the form of pressure and stress. It only makes one confined to involving the self as per a situation and in ways needed to tackle the competitor. Therefore, these souls need to divert their attention and aggression in doing something exciting. This can include travel and exploration, fitness goals, adventure, and sporting activities, where there is not just plenty of excitement but also some healthy competition.

Chapter 23
SELF-CENTRED SOULS

We have all come across people who can endlessly talk about themselves, regardless of where they are or with whom they are. People who love to make the self the centre of attention or the centre point of any conversation and express their likes, dislikes, opinions, and thoughts without being probed or prompted. Basically, they can effortlessly connect just about anything and everything to their own choices, preferences, opinions etc.

Then there are some who tend to make a big deal of even the slightest inconvenience to them. Such people are so sensitive and reactive to external influences that they make a lot of hue and cry at every opportunity.

Both these categories consist of souls who are so caught up with the self that they attach very little importance to anyone or anything else other than the self. For them, the entire world and life, in general, revolve only around their own needs, desires, ambitions, achievements, failures, comforts, discomforts, likes, dislikes, joys, and sorrow.

Driven by the mantra of 'I, me, myself', these souls are so self-obsessed that putting up with them can be immensely challenging. But the thing that prompts these souls towards this kind of extreme behaviour is not any kind of arrogance or pride but a greater inner vacuum, which is certainly not easy to read.

Self-centred souls, at times, can be mistaken as narcissists but unlike the latter, they do not lack empathy or seek compliments, they don't pick on others, or think they are right. Instead, these souls simply remain too preoccupied with the noise in their head, which largely revolves around their own self. So, they could be listening to you in a conversation but their mind will be racing to the next thought about the self that can be brought up in the conversation. This can be something about their likes, dislikes, or their own experiences.

Another prominent trait of these souls is that they like to be dramatic in their expression. They like to exaggerate things when explaining them from their own standpoint. And they express themselves with a sense of urgency. Though if a conversation doesn't give them the room and space to fill in their own ideas, they can get bored easily. You'll often find these souls not letting you complete the sentence in a conversation and abruptly intrude with their own line of thinking. This is because all they want is attention and plenty of it. They want to be acknowledged and heard. And they are solely concerned with their own needs, desires, and interests. Nothing external influences them much because they are highly preoccupied with their own mental conversations, ideas, obsessions, and priorities.

Also, a conversation with self-centred souls can be completely one-sided and you'll find them losing interest if they have to play the role of a listener. Therefore, putting up with them can also get frustrating and to some, they can even come across as selfish but there is also a childlike innocence in them and they are easy to read and transparent. They don't have any secret agendas and they certainly aren't diplomatic. They simply want to be addressed and heard. Also, all that talk revolving around the self is often just a confidence-building measure from their end, which serves the purpose of assuring the self of their own importance and well-being.

An important question to consider here is what is the thing that makes them so identified with the self or self-centred? The fact is that their apparent self-centeredness comes from a deep-rooted need for self-preservation and protection, which surfaces occasionally. This also makes these souls somewhat unsure of themselves and hence, they have this great need to overemphasise the self and dwell too much in their own thought process, behaviour, likes and dislikes, etc. Their inability to see anything beyond the self also makes them extra cautious and extra sensitive towards the self. Therefore, any slightest threat to their gains, comforts, or survival can push these souls into a state of anxiety and nervousness.

These souls also have come with the desire to restore their independence and individuality and prioritise their needs, wishes, and beliefs. The cause that led to the culmination of this desire can be found in their past lives. It could be that in their past lives, they were deprived of equality and balance in personal equations or that there was too much self-neglect owing to enmeshment or co-dependency in relationships. It could also be that their unselfishness in their previous lifetimes cost them their individuality as these souls were either too relationship-driven or lost themselves in the other. Perhaps there was drama and trauma in their relationships that created a need to find their own meaning and purpose. Or perhaps, they got so involved with others that they lost the connection with the self. It is also possible that these souls remained too cautious in the past and made personal compromises to balance and accommodate their relationships and keep other people happy and pleased. Maybe they went along with people and situations and felt a sense of emptiness due to their compromising nature.

And it is this emptiness or vacuum that calls to be addressed now. It is what makes these souls go off balance and overdo things for the sake of safeguarding their individuality. In short, these souls are here to reclaim their sense of self and authority. They are here to shine individually in whatever capacity and establish their identity.

The Karmic Mandates for Self-Centred Souls

These are the three essential present-life karmic mandates for self-centred souls:

1. **Develop individuality and assertiveness**

   These souls need to create a healthy self-image and for that, they need to build their individuality and authority. The best way to rediscover the self and create a healthy self-image is by being independent and enterprising, focusing on self-efforts, inculcating leadership and entrepreneurial skills, and participating in creative or humanitarian work. Also, the more they learn to operate through their own intelligence, skills, and talents, and the more they assert their strengths through what they do, the sooner they will be able to establish their individuality and authority.

   So, these souls need to give a voice to their ideas, talents, and skills, which may have remained suppressed in their past lives. They need to give the self the necessary permission to express itself freely and pursue what they desire with utmost freedom. But they also need to practically execute their thoughts and ideas in some sort of concrete work, rather than keeping them confined to one-sided conversations. Basically, they need more action than talk in order to feel more powerful in life.

2. **Interdependence instead of co-dependence**

For self-centred souls, it's good to have healthy emotional boundaries in their relationships. They shouldn't be codependent in any way (psychological, emotional, or financial) and not become overbearing or selfish in relationships. The reason why this is an important mandate is because healthy relationships are needed to develop and nurture one's own personality. Without relationships or healthy human equations, one only gets more obsessive and delusional about the self. Therefore, these souls need to allow others to be equally present in daily interactions and respect their viewpoints.

In their past lives, they may have prioritised relationships, so now, it is important for them to achieve a healthy balance between the self and the other. Operating through an interdependent nature can help them maintain their own inner balance as well as the significance and sanctity of their relationships. While they don't need to compromise in any way, they need to ensure that their selfishness doesn't make others feel rejected or deprived.

To conclude, competitive souls need to open up and speak their mind, but they also need to listen and make the other person feel loved and respected. Relationships, in fact, can become a wonderful means for these souls to express the self as well as understand the other side of the human story.

3. **Build more excitement**

Since these souls may have lacked the excitement of

their own journey in the past, they have been called to experiment with new adventures and break away from conventional roles. They need to do something that excites them and helps them enjoy a sense of exclusivity. This could be anything that helps channel their urge to be the centre of attention into a more positive and concrete direction. Something that involves passion, risk-taking, adventure, being inventive, and pioneering and also helps bring some amount of recognition.

So, the final karmic mandate for these souls is to break out of routines and conventional lives in order to go on a journey that leads to self-discovery, excitement, and joy of living life independently.

Chapter 24
CREATIVE SOULS

Freedom is the keyword that describes creative souls. Freedom to choose, freedom to express, and freedom to create what they really want. And this freedom arises from a sense of independence, which most creative souls clearly enjoy about almost everything in life. Also, it is not hard to decipher that these souls have a distinctive and unique thought process along with capabilities that are truly uncommon.

In terms of their nature, creative souls run purely on inspiration and intuition and feel driven to come up with something original and new. Their deep sense of originality coupled with an absolute need to produce individual magic pushes them towards some truly bold, out-of-the-box, and extraordinary feats. This also makes them reject the stereotypes and opt for something that others are unlikely to engage in.

Creative souls find it difficult to follow any set norms, definition, or pattern and instead are unconventional as well as experimental in their choices. What may be considered a convenient or popular route to success or what might be the most widely pursued set of activities usually fails to capture their interest. These souls cannot relate to herd mentality or do something because it is widely accepted as a safe bet. They simply cannot fit into the conventional style of living and pursuing things, primarily because they like to create life in each moment and not take up a clichéd route that unfolds life in a repetitive way. In short, there is only one way for these souls and that is their own way.

The reason what may be certified as 'normal' by the vast majority comes across as boring to these souls is because they prefer to be challenged and think out of the box, rather than do something that lacks risk-taking, originality, and creative gratification. These souls like to create their own paths, their own set of activities, and go for new and different pursuits in life. Pursuits that have a sense of uniqueness about them, have scope for newness and creation, and have plenty of room to showcase individual skills and talents, which are essentially their driving force.

As mentioned, these souls like doing things that match their creative vision, suit their comfort level, and allow them to go at their own pace. Given the unpredictable nature of the work and activities they like to indulge in, they do not like being pushed around. And even though their penchant for perfection and creative expression can sometimes come across as a bit painful and impractical, most creative souls tend to show the kind of perseverance that is often hard to beat.

Creativity for these souls is not just an occupation or activity, it is, in fact, a way of life. So, they have a unique approach to whatever they are doing and like to use this creativity in expressing their inner talent. They look at things imaginatively and give a personal touch to all their activities. This is something that makes them relish any sort of activity, regardless of how mundane it may be.

Since creation is their true calling in life, creative souls tend to stretch themselves as far as they possibly can in order to express the self creatively. One could find them doing the simplest of things quite differently and with a sense of involvement and enjoyment, which comes through giving some bit of their creative expression to each of their chosen activities. One can say that everything that these souls do, they do it creatively. There is no other way that they understand and cannot be expected to deal with things in a mechanical and unoriginal manner.

Creative souls are what they are due to their significant levels of passion. They can be extremely or moderately passionate about things but they just cannot do something without feeling passionate about it. Especially, when it is their major occupation or the activity that takes up most of their time. It has to be something they are passionate about. And, they mostly like doing things on their own and without help and guidance from others. Too much external influence or pressure can stifle their capabilities and thwart their progress.

Another defining characteristic of creative souls is their proclivity to devise their own method or style and stamp their uniqueness on whatever they undertake. They have the capability to ingeniously combine life's raw potential with ideas from their imaginative and inventive mind in order to create something different, something that evokes a sense of delight and wonder. They also like to put a bit of their own personality because, for creative souls, their work is not separate from their self. This helps them derive a unique identity and they cherish this aspect the most. All in all, an intention to be different, coupled with deep curiosity and a keen desire to discover new and untapped aspects of life, keeps these souls going.

Interestingly, although creative souls have the most constructive and original mind, it instinctively lacks the intensive cerebral, technical, mathematical, and scientific capability. Perhaps, the same was already developed in their past lives and it now needs to be somewhat passive, in order to let their imaginative and intuitive capability surface. Or perhaps, these souls need to continue a journey that was started in a previous birth and would end only once the creative side of their personality is fully developed.

Since most creative souls are emotional, sensitive, and possessive in nature, they may need to heal from past life difficulties or even traumas, which often lead to such qualities. And so, they have been given a role where they can immerse themselves fully and derive a sense of soothing joy from their work. Often, their work can be therapeutic and can lead them to blissful surrender. And these souls, who may be on a healing journey need to lose the self in such activity. Therefore, each time they sing, paint, draw, write, dance, or create something, they can experience rejuvenation and heightened peace.

It is also possible that these souls need to heal the self from the dreariness of mechanical routines, which dominated their past lives. So now, they are being asked to connect with the lively, expressive, intuitive, imaginative, and inspired side of their personality. This is also the spiritual aspect as creativity cannot be achieved without tapping into one's spiritual nature comprising of love, peace, and compassion.

The Karmic Mandates for Creative Souls

The three essential present-life karmic mandates for creative souls include:

1. **Renew their spirit**

   In the case of all creative souls, their key mandate in life is to recharge and renew their spirit through devotion and surrender to what they do. In other words, they are here to enjoy the fullness of life. And since all forms of creative expression, be it music, art, dance, performing arts, writing, cooking, painting, designing, gardening, etc., fully involve, excite, and nourish the doer, it is a great way for creative souls to achieve this mandate. Such activities will help them break the clutter of routine thoughts and experience renewed energy.

So, be it their work or any activity, the creativity in their life is sure to act as an inspirational and healing medium which, in turn, can lead to a positive transformation. It is meant to help them cleanse and dissolve the heavy energy of any past trauma or the dullness and weariness of mechanically driven lives in the past. Creative activities, therefore, are good medicine for their soul. It also helps them express their sensitive side in a more positive and powerful way and share their truth and their stories in a way that isn't just therapeutic for them but also insightful and inspirational for the audience.

2. **Develop spiritually**

Another important karmic mandate for these souls is to develop spiritually, though not by taking the conventional route to spirituality, but through the use and application of their intuitive powers. As we all know, intuition has a huge role to play in any creative work. Without intuition, the magic of creativity cannot be achieved. And the more one uses their intuition, the more powerful it becomes. We also know that creative activities have a meditative effect on the doer. This is because all creative work harmonises the mind, body, and spirit of a person and elicits such precise attention that the process itself becomes a means of meditation and relaxation. That is, it becomes a way to silence one's mind and energise the intuition.

And energising the intuition amounts to the gain of spiritual powers because when we connect with our intuition, we reach a state of higher consciousness or what is also known as soul consciousness. And the more one remains in such a state, the more one rises spiritually. So creative souls are here to grow spiritually through the power and use of their intuition.

3. **Live a higher purpose**

Creative souls have a karmic mandate to create a sense of beauty and joy in the world.

They are here to break the monotony and the repetitive patterns that tend to make life mechanical and boring and create new flavours, new varieties, new choices, and add new and unexplored dimensions to human life which are most necessary for evolution. They are also here to reflect the power of self-expression, the power of originality, and to introduce new and more stimulating ways of being as well as doing things.

It can be said that most creative souls, in one way or the other, are the healers of this world. In the sense that for everyone, it is always the creative side of life that tends to recharge and refuel the spirit. It has the power to light up one's emotions and imagination while evoking a definite sense of excitement, peace, joy, and even pathos. And then sometimes, creative work can be so powerful that it can create quite a stir within us and move us to discover something extraordinary within the self. So, creativity and healing go hand in hand. And any creative work isn't just a means to raise the vibration of the doer but also of those who can relate to their work.

Also, any new creative invention or innovation in any field of work always brings with it a lot of excitement apart from being of significant value to humanity. Therefore, it is not wrong to say that creative souls do have a higher mission in life! They are here to execute a higher purpose.

Chapter 25
ENLIGHTENED SOULS

From time immemorial, enlightened souls have been around and played an important role in raising the awareness and harmony of the planet. Their empowering presence has been rendering a silent service to all the other souls and positively affecting not just the world but the entire existence.

It is important to note that enlightened souls are never quite like the stereotypical god-men or preachers. They are neither supporters nor proponents of any philosophy, ideology, or religious path. Also, none of their words or actions is meant for attention-grabbing purposes. The fact is that purely through the way they manage their own energies, these souls add purity and positivity to the energy of the planet. They radiate unseen power and introduce other souls to a more elevated mental, emotional, psychological, and spiritual state of being.

So, we can say that enlightened souls are energy transformers since they operate through higher consciousness and influence their surroundings through their powerful vibrations. And those who connect with them or come in contact with them are bound to feel this rare energy, which tends to create a definite sense of peace and quell stress and worry. Their serene, encouraging, and energising presence is especially helpful for those people who are in search of emotional stability, mental serenity, intellectual clarity, and spiritual calmness.

There are countless stories that depict ancient saints and mystics doing something magical to people who approached them with turbulent energy and a restless mind. Something that not only gave these people a sense of relief but also helped them feel renewed and rejuvenated. And this transformation usually came in the form of a blessing, which we all know is nothing but a transmission of energy from a high-frequency soul to a low-frequency soul. This energy is often so pure and powerful that it has the ability to counter all kinds of negativity and bring about a profound sense of healing. Let's take a closer look at this transformation process.

We all know that two people interact not just through words and actions but also through their energies. In actuality, energy is nothing but a sum total of one's inner state or one's accumulated thoughts, feelings, and emotions. This energy has a vibration and when two people interact, they come in contact with each other's vibrations. And how they feel about each other depends on the quality of their individual vibration.

This explains why, at times, we may feel uncomfortable in the company of certain people, despite their positive actions and carefully articulated words. Or why we may feel comfortable with certain people who, without making any effort, tend to make us feel good and reassured.

This goes on to show that energy has more power to significantly impact our feelings than words or actions. Therefore, any interaction with enlightened souls is likely to generate a peaceful and happy feeling within us. They attain high-quality energy through the stillness of their minds, steady inner peace, a sense of deep contentment with life, and highly detached intellect, which neither judges nor gets too involved with the noise of the world around them. Hence, their presence has the most enlivening and inspiring influence on others.

Another reason for their powerful presence is that there is rarely a shade of turbulence within enlightened souls, which results from their deep and unfailing trust in life as well as in the universal forces. It also comes from not wanting to control life and having the willingness to accept things just as they are. And the foundation for all these characteristics is a nurturing consciousness that is permanently stationed in the non-material and a spiritually attuned thought process. As such, enlightened souls, through their unique sensibility, participate in life with complete non-interference, unconditional surrender, and relentless gratitude.

Enlightened souls are also often the brightest minds. Their wisdom comes from their profound understanding of the self and life. This immense wisdom can be seen in their impeccable conduct and demeanour and their ever-unruffled state of being, which inspires others towards seeking awareness and self-sufficiency in life.

Another common feature of enlightened souls is that they do not spend time anticipating the future or dwelling in the past. For them, the present is all that there is. Therefore, they neither waste energy by thinking more than what is necessary nor by escaping the present moment. Their absolute submission to the present gives them unmatched clarity and greater insight, which help them create harmony.

These souls may not necessarily be into any conventional religious or spiritual practice, but they live life through their spiritual nature of peace, power, compassion, humility, love, and happiness. Though the most important spiritual practice, which these souls adhere to, is living in the now.

They are never really detached from the now and this keeps them in harmony with life and with anyone who comes in contact with them. It also helps them maintain their inner equilibrium and their ever-empowered inner state.

Since we have covered the primary characteristics of enlightened souls, let's now look at what makes these souls who they are.

In their past lifetimes, these souls may have been self-sacrificing and devoted to a higher ideal. Their deeds may have been motivated by compassion, kindness, and the purpose of human welfare. And through their character, their awakened state of being, and their noble deeds, they may have merged with their own divinity.

It is also evident that enlightened souls have spent many previous lifetimes dissolving the ego. So, not only do they have a low burden of karma but also the maturity that helps them to avoid accumulating more karma. After all, it is the ego that makes us build karmic debts. As we have covered before, ego-driven behaviour is the primary factor that complicates human equations and deeds and creates serious debts of karma. Thus, the ego becomes a major obstacle in one's spiritual growth as it takes us away from our spiritual nature of love, peace, and happiness; qualities that enlightened souls have understood as their true nature and hence, have progressed on their spiritual journey by crossing all hurdles of the ego.

And having already achieved a considerable amount of familiarity with the higher truth, it is highly probable that enlightened souls may have spent a significant number of past lives devoted to a practical exploration and application of truth. It is also likely that experimenting with the higher truth may have added greater understanding and substance to their being and helped them transform into blissful and unwavering personalities. After all, only when we use the truth in life situations can we understand its true power and become truly enlightened.

And we are all here to know this truth and understand our deeper self through this truth. Also, our real purpose, and the nature of this existence. Therefore, the one who manages to decode and grasp the answers to these most pertinent questions has no reason to feel dissatisfied, curious, anxious, restless, or confused. Such a soul earns enlightenment along with an awareness of self, life, and everything connected to it. This awareness automatically converts into inexhaustible peace and utmost maturity, which are two of the most fundamental characteristics of enlightened beings.

Imagine a soul with no questions, no dilemmas, no confusion at all, a soul who has the answers to the little as well as big questions about the self and life. Will there not be complete stillness and peace inside such a soul? For restlessness only comes when one is totally perplexed or lost or has several unanswered questions about the self and life. Thus, we can say that enlightened souls, through their understanding of the higher truth, have achieved the highest mandate of human life and they are now here to make others aware of this truth.

The Karmic Mandates for Enlightened Souls

From our above analysis, the important karmic mandates for enlightened souls are pretty evident. They are:

1. **Touch lives**

   Enlightened souls are here to touch lives and bring comfort, order, harmony, and healing. They are here to participate in life and offer their immaculate stillness and empowering energy to the world. They are also here to exemplify the power of being present and living life in the now which is perhaps, the greatest spiritual practice, which differentiates the enlightened beings from the unenlightened. And even though such a practice may seem too ordinary and simple, it has the extraordinary ability to dissolve the ego. And enlightened souls have attained this wisdom in their past lives and they are now here to make others realise this truth in order to overcome their individual egos.

2. **Spread awareness of the truth**

Enlightened souls are not here to teach some sacred, ancient wisdom, or propound conventional methods of meditation. They are also not here to create a philosophy or a path to spirituality or create a following or enchant the world with their wisdom and oratory skills. For enlightened souls understand that the ultimate truth is above all these things and it can only be experienced by surrendering the ego and through the complete understanding and acceptance of life, the way it functions, its practical lessons, and the profound wisdom it imparts. They are here to teach the real meaning and value of harmonising with the experience and wisdom of life.

Enlightened souls are not here to teach a lesson on truth, they are here to share the truth. The truth of life, of the ego and its many evils. Truth that is stored in their subconscious memory and has been attained after spending many lifetimes working on their ego. Ego which is the cause of all ignorance and the decline of one's spiritual powers. So, enlightened souls are not here to preach something or to continue the legacy of some spiritual organisation and group. They are here to awaken ignorant minds, through sharing their own truth and by making this truth be felt in their presence.

3. **Help raise the vibration of the planet**

Since the energy and vibration of enlightened souls have a positive influence on others, their next important mandate becomes to create a harmonious balance in the collective energy of the planet. Something, they can do through their own inner peace and tranquillity, which may be lying dormant in many people or may seem inaccessible due to a lack of self-awareness and an over-active ego. This is the reason why when such people come in contact with enlightened beings, they feel charged with peace and tranquillity. Yet, this peace and tranquillity aren't transmitted to them by those who are enlightened. Instead, these qualities are already within them which become alive and invigorated when they are in a positively charged energy field, such as that of enlightened souls.

So, the last mandate for enlightened souls is to silently push others towards greater self-awareness and towards the awareness of their inner peace and power that's important to raise their own vibration as well as the collective vibration of the planet. Also, to bring about any kind of positive transformation in any soul, peace is the first big necessity. For it is only peace, which when restored in our soul personality, can help us evolve to our higher self.

Chapter 26

IMPORTANCE OF HONOURING KARMIC MANDATES

No matter how much we like to believe that this life is all we have or this human form is who we are, the fact remains that each human form is just a role assigned to us and each life is only a small event in the long and eternal journey of a soul. A journey where a soul rises and falls and then rises again to its highest and purest state. And so, each life has the potential to become the most significant event in the journey of a soul as it provides the opportunity to know, experience, and understand itself.

But the point to be kept in mind here is that it is just an opportunity and not the ultimate reality of a soul. This life or this role is just a means to the end. Therefore, there really is no point in getting too identified with life or the role that we are playing in our human forms, as they are finite and temporary. Though what's permanent is the growth and evolution that comes with every role, provided that one makes the necessary effort to understand the true purpose of a given role and look deeper into their respective role to understand the karmic mandate attached to it. A mandate we need to honour for our own spiritual progress.

After all, we are souls in a human form, playing a certain role that has been given to us in order to dissolve our fears, doubts, complexities, insecurities, unhappiness, regrets, misgivings, hurt, pain, and emotional burden, all of which are the creation of the ego and destroy our spiritual powers of peace, happiness, love, compassion, courage, and humility and makes us lose connection with our true self, our spiritual self. And with each life, we get an opportunity to reconnect with our true self through a given role. In fact, every single thing that is associated with life, from birth to death, is just for the sake of learning and understanding more about the self, so that we progress and transform into more powerful spiritual energies.

But we get so involved with the façade and become so mesmerised by the world of physicality and forms and so captivated by this instant gratification and fleeting joy of sensory comfort that it takes no time for us to forget who we really are and for what reason we are here. Sometimes, we live our life so unconsciously that we lose a lot of spiritual powers and thus, accumulate a lot of karmic debts. Basically, the more unconsciously and aimlessly we live, the more debts of karma we create. And the more we operate out of the ego and tendencies manifested by the ego or tendencies that are the opposite of our spiritual nature, the more karmic burden we gain. After all, ego not only destroys our inner powers but also impacts our relationships and external situations and circumstances. It makes us respond incorrectly to life and people and thereby gets us entangled in karmic complications. And it is this burden of karma that adds darker layers to a soul's energy and makes it attract lifetimes that are complex and challenging. It also delays the soul's evolution and growth.

To recapitulate, the five primary factors that make us increase our burden of karma are:

- Egoic conditioning of the mind
- Excessive material or role identification and loss of connection with our spiritual self
- Loss of our intrinsic powers
- Unconscious living
- Lack of self-awareness

Therefore, it is important to understand our higher truth, our higher purpose, and our higher mandate in life. This way, we save the self from getting further entangled in karmic knots and return to our higher self.

Karmic Mandates Empower Destiny

Another important thing to understand about our karmic mandates is that they are the means to positively alter our destiny and change the course of our life by taking charge and doing what is needed. They are there to help us create a powerful destiny and remove any obstacles along the way.

As discussed in the previous chapters, we are a sum total of our intentions, thoughts, words, emotions, feelings, and deeds. Our inner qualities and inner state attract our outer situations and experiences, which amount to destiny. Also, what we live out as destiny in a given time frame is only a response of that inner being to everything external. For the point is not what we face in life; rather, it is how we deal with it, and that's our destiny!

Destiny is not what we can read through planetary alignments or some prophecy; it is not what the stars have in store for us. In fact, our destiny is created by our everyday attitude towards life and this is the most decisive factor in determining what we are likely to face because we attract what we are. And our karmic mandates are for the purpose of empowering who we are. Hence, they help us alter our destiny in a positive way.

We can be in the most hopeless or difficult circumstances, but if we put in the effort to align with our true mandate for a given life, we are bound to alter our state of mind as well as our experiences. For our karmic mandate is our pathway to a higher inner state, a state of greater self-awareness, self-control, and self-sufficiency through which we can create our own destiny. Our karmic mandate helps us respond to life with maturity and this empowers destiny.

So, if someone thinks of the self as less fortunate or feels that their experience of life is not so joyful and that their inner state is not so peaceful, blissful, powerful, or grateful, then adhering to their karmic mandate can help bring about the necessary growth and change.

Karmic Mandates Are the Gateway to Growth

We must remember that we are souls on a human journey, and we have come into this world of forms to manage the self better. We have come to regain our lost powers, settle old debts of karma, and not create any new debts. These things happen naturally when we understand not just our roles correctly but also the karmic mandate attached to them. Understanding and honouring our karmic mandate means that we are:

- Making the necessary effort to fill up the deficiencies in our deeper personality
- Becoming better beings
- Doing what we have come to do in life and not questioning it
- Empowering the self in ways that make us play our form-based role effectively
- Settling pending debts of karma
- Avoiding more debts

This happens because each karmic mandate is there to help a soul dissolve undesirable tendencies and patterns of behaviour, and once a soul starts honouring the mandate, it means that everything else falls into place.

Also, a soul will continue to take on different human forms, different roles, and key mandates in order mature, evolve, and align with spiritual consciousness. And till this happens, a soul will always need a role to fulfil a specific karmic mandate because, for every soul, the main purpose of life is to achieve consciousness expansion and growth. And this can't be achieved just by living a life or playing a particular role. Instead, it requires adhering to the true karmic mandate that comes with a given role.

So, karma being action and mandate meaning the official order of the universe, every karmic mandate for a soul is the primary action that it needs to perform in the given role. Till this mandate is honoured to the fullest, a soul will not achieve the true purpose of the role and may need to return in another lifetime to a similar role, in order to complete the unfinished task. And the sooner this mandate is lived and fulfilled, the quicker a soul is able to gain a different role, which holds greater growth prospects for the soul.

Karmic Mandates and the Bigger Shift

Honouring our karmic mandate holds greater significance because:

- It helps us heal from the past and erase soul recordings that are disempowering.
- It also helps raise our positive energy, which enables us to progress on our spiritual path.

An important point to note is that when we honour our karmic mandate, or when we raise our inner powers and positivity, we also make a big difference to other people's energy. This happens because when we reflect a positive change in our own attitude, outlook, and behaviour, it permeates into the lives of other people and inspires them to grow and evolve.

Here, one needs to understand that words do not matter as much as we think they do! We can say a thousand positive and inspirational things to others but they will never be able to feel the power of those words until they experience them. They may listen to those words and appreciate them, but they will not be able to absorb them and feel moved to bring a positive shift in their own consciousness. So, it's our energy that needs to do the talking and not our words.

And when we honour our karmic mandate, we work on the prospects of growth and with growth, we become instruments of change in this world. This, in fact, is also the way we create good karma. For karma is nothing but an exchange of energy. It could be an exchange with the animate world or even with the inanimate world. For example, if we operate through a negative set of tendencies while making money and use greed and dishonesty, then what we are giving out to this inanimate object (money) is energy, which is negative. Therefore, what will return to us is liquid wealth with an energy that will neither help us feel grateful nor satisfied nor will such wealth bring good health and happiness.

We can see this phenomenon in the world around us. There are some people who may be wealthy, but their homes and hearts may lack peace, happiness, and health. This is simply because the tendencies used to make their money failed to create the right energy to attract money that could give them peace, health, joy, and satisfaction. This means that if we want peace, fulfilment, happiness, and health through our wealth, we need to earn it with a more positive set of tendencies and intent.

What is also very important to remember is that karma or the energy that we give out returns to us as our own destiny. And what we experience through our destiny, in return, shapes our tendencies. So, something definitely changes when we, as souls, play our part in a physical form. Whether we do it consciously or unconsciously, we are likely to influence a change upon the self as well as in the world and people around us, because who we are deep within is the energy that we are sending out! Energy, that has both positive and negative currents, depending on the quality of our tendencies. And these currents reach people and things and create an experience for others as well as for the self. In fact, our energy impacts every cell in our body and each and everything around us. Similarly, other people's energy also has an impact on us and on this world. Therefore, we can conclude that our tendencies determine our consciousness, which, in turn, determines our energy, our vibe, or what others feel about us. And it is this energy that has an impact on us and on everything and everyone around us.

This explains why a person honouring their true karmic mandate can become an instrument of that all-important positive change! The truth is that a single person can set off a chain reaction, which will not just help raise the collective consciousness but also the all-important energy or vibration of the planet. And to create a peaceful and happier planet, all we need to do is work towards our own positive transformation and evolution as coded in our individual mandate. Once we are able to identify with a particular soul category, we must make all efforts to adhere to our given mandate and become instruments of a positive change. And this starts with showing the intent to know what is beyond the physical self! For intent, as we all know, is true karma.

Therefore, once we set this karma in action, all the help from the universe is sent our way. Because the universe is forever present in our journey and is always ready to lend us help, provided that we show keenness to awaken to our true self and seek a conscious living.

On other hand, if we continue living ignorantly and are led by our egoic conditioning, the universe becomes a passive observer in our journey, and it will remain so, unless of course, we send out the energy showing our readiness to know our deeper truth and a strong willingness to part from our egoist, conditioned self! Hence, by observing, questioning, and introspecting, we can go beyond all the material superficiality and are more likely to receive help from the universe in the form of information, insights, intuition, and people to honour our true mandate.

But first, we need to realise that our karmic mandate is not just about this mundane life or its day-to-day dynamics, chores, businesses, needs, insecurities, ambitions, desires, or even our conscious thoughts and imagination. It is not singularly aligned with our job, career, homes, family or friends, dreams, desires, debts, struggles, tragedies, triumphs, competitions, achievements, or failures, or even our routines, rituals, religion, culture, society, faith, gender, etc. Rather, our karmic mandate is deeply connected to our mental, psychological, emotional, and subconscious reality, which when combined together, amounts to our spiritual self. Simply put, our karmic mandate is connected to our response to life and how we deal with life and manage our inner powers and virtues in the process. It also shows what we need to do as spiritual beings in order to progress on our spiritual path. And once our spiritual side starts flourishing, our physical state is also bound to do well!

SECTION 3

In the next few chapters of the book, we try and understand the cause and effect of our state of being. We will understand all those factors that will help us decode the personal mystery, power, and inner mechanism of a soul. Factors that not just contribute to how a soul progresses through its human journey but also to its eventual advancement in terms of consciousness expansion and growth.

Here, the readers will get to understand what makes a soul essay its human role effectively and discover ways that will help them play their individual roles well. In short, this section explores our inner truth in greater detail and brings to light the more important aspects beneath the surface reality that help us understand Why We Are Who We Are, and how can we become better.

Chapter 27

TWO STATES AND A SOUL

In order to decode our personal mystery and understand why we are who we are, we need to look within. We need to relate to our inner state which is the key factor in determining our nature, how we lead our life, and our experiences.

As souls, we operate through two very different states. These two states are a part of our soul personality and they drive our choices, our reactions, our decisions, and everything internal that connects us to the external life. Out of the two states, one is our natural state. It is a state where we are more relaxed and in our comfort zone as this lets us operate through our natural self which includes tendencies like peace, love, happiness, power, and harmony. The tendency of peace further builds comfort, calmness, equanimity, and bliss, while love further creates compassion, affection, and oneness. On the other hand, happiness leads to joy, cheer, contentment, and gratitude and power within a soul makes it fearless, determined, confident, cooperative, giving, and trusting and finally, harmony brings balance along with a sense of optimism and hope.

Such tendencies emerge spontaneously from our soul personality and do not disturb our inner environment. They, instead, make us more positive and empowered and also lead us to a more balanced behaviour and inner stability, which help us attract experiences that are pleasant in nature.

This state tends to keep our energy light and free-flowing and never causes any imbalance or disturbance in our inner chemistry. It also makes us feel mentally, emotionally, psychologically, and even physically healthy. In fact, every soul constantly likes to be in this state, where it can effortlessly respond to life with purity and positivity, which are a byproduct of inner peace, happiness, and strength. Thus, we can say that the natural state is the most ideal state for a soul to operate out of.

The second state is an entirely different state. It is, in fact, the opposite of the first and so, it can be defined as an unnatural state. When in this state, the tendencies through which a soul responds to and experiences life are offshoots of the ego. This includes anger, fear, jealousy, vanity, and greed. And once again, we need to understand that anger is not mere anger. It builds aggression, stress, tension, and violence within us and creates pain, hurt, and bitterness. On the other hand, fear creates low self-esteem, self-doubt, insecurity, lack of trust, confusion, anxiety, and trauma, while vanity gives way to narcissism, arrogance, dominance, stubbornness, etc. Also, jealousy creates pessimism, suspicion, resentment, and greed, which, in turn, create dissatisfaction, restlessness, dishonesty, and ambition.

Basically, all these qualities combine into tendencies, which make us totally uncomfortable, turbulent, and unstable. And this is because they clash with our natural state as they are not in sync with what we as souls prefer naturally. They create a sort of aberration in our responses and behaviour and never quite let us be at ease. At times, these tendencies even result in temporary insanity as they detach us from our natural state. And at times, they can get so overpowering that we start identifying with them as our natural qualities. And this is when our unconscious behaviour starts manifesting.

This happens because, in our unnatural state, we are neither operating at will nor thinking and feeling right at most times. We remain perplexed and tired as our inner powers and capacity get drained while combating thoughts, feelings, and emotions, which aren't natural. And this causes extreme helplessness and discomfort. It also results in reactive behaviour and negative attitude, which makes our experience of life quite difficult to accept and creates disharmony with life. In such a state, life feels like a long-drawn battle where one is overcome by a sense of weariness. We also lose the ability to look within and spend most of our time seeing life as the enemy and combating people and situations, which we consider as the reason for our problems. The combat also arises owing to the fact that in our unnatural state, we always feel imbalanced and have to deal with intrusions that hinder our natural way of functioning.

Though in our natural state, we operate through the more empowering qualities of peace and happiness and respond to life through inner stability, which effortlessly creates an outer balance. This natural state is essential if we want to stay in harmony with life and focus on progress and areas of self-development and growth rather than being in a constant warzone. Therefore, when we, as souls, are in our natural state, it can be said that we are living consciously, while in our unnatural state, we tend to live unconsciously as we operate through an inner personality that's self-destructive.

An important point that needs greater emphasis here is that whichever state a soul operates out of, whichever state is more actively attached to its behaviour and experiences, with time, the tendencies of that particular state become an integral part of its personality and pretty soon, the soul starts identifying that particular state as its natural state. Thus, if someone is accustomed to using anger too frequently, then he or she will soon start believing that anger is fine or that anger is natural. And the more they use anger or any other quality of their unnatural state, the more these qualities will grow and become a part of their personality. On the contrary, if they choose to stay peaceful even in the most instigating and disturbing situations, if they choose to simply observe things without labelling or judging them and reacting to them, then it will be very difficult for such souls to adopt anger or any unnatural tendency as a means to express themselves.

So, it's important to remember that the tendencies we choose to use more frequently determine the state through which we operate and this state eventually becomes our identity. And it is this identity or our soul personality that gets deeply embedded in our subconscious mind and is carried forward into future lifetimes.

Therefore, the more energy we invest in our natural state, the more our thoughts, feelings, and actions stay aligned with our natural state, the more power we will gain and create a better identity and life experiences for the self. We will also secure a better future by doing so.

We need to realise that the purpose of any given life is to build the right identity for the self. And for this, we need to understand our true self correctly and accept that our unnatural state is flawed and unhealthy, as only then can we live more consciously. And upon enquiring, should our unnatural state seem more active, it needs to be corrected in the present lifetime. As only then can we return to our natural state and our higher self.

Chapter 28

CONSCIOUSNESS HOLDS THE KEY

As discussed in the previous chapter, a soul needs to pay careful attention to the self in order to know the state it mostly operates out of and only then can it also apply the knowledge and means that can bring a sense of permanence to its natural state. But if we explore a soul's natural and unnatural states a bit more, a few questions come up.

- What is it that determines the state or the tendencies through which a soul operates?
- What is it that makes a soul choose a given set of tendencies?
- How do the natural and unnatural states co-exist in a person?
- And what really is the basis of one's behaviour?

These are some key questions that need to be asked to understand the very basis of the two states of the soul. And the answer to all these questions lies in a single word—consciousness.

Consciousness can also be understood as awareness and it is what a soul carries over lifetimes. It changes with time and with the ways in which it encounters life, but consciousness plays a decisive role in determining the state of the soul. So, when a being and its human form come together, it is consciousness which takes control of how we (the being or the soul) while existing in a physical form (the body) would respond to life. Meaning, how we deal with the events, circumstances, and situations that come along the way and subsequently what we become in the process are all dependent on our consciousness. In short, our soul's tendencies, personality, and behaviour, all originate from consciousness.

In other words, consciousness is the true strength of a soul as it makes a soul operate either through its natural or unnatural state. And just as we have two different states through which a soul operates, we also have two different aspects which consciousness identifies with.

The first aspect that the consciousness or awareness identifies with is the body and this covers the physical, material, or tangible dimension. While the second aspect consciousness identifies with is the soul, which includes everything spiritual, metaphysical, and intangible. The physical aspect would amount to everything that is temporary and dependent on external factors; basically, things that are erratic and transient in nature. On the contrary, the spiritual aspect consists of things that are real, permanent, and comfortable.

However, once in a human form, consciousness tends to identify more with the body and things that are physical, material, and tangible. It largely remains centred around these things and this way, it gradually begins to give less attention to what is relevant to the being and instead places more importance on temporary and foreign things. And as our physical form matures, our consciousness identifies more and more with the physical and material and less and less with the spiritual. And soon, we lose the memory of our true self, i.e., the spiritual self.

But why is it that the more our consciousness identifies with forms, the more we begin to see things through the eyes of the world? This is due to concepts and labels that give rise to the ego. And it happens because the conceptual understanding of life or the label-driven existence limits our mental horizon and keeps us locked in a set of beliefs. The more we operate through these limited beliefs, the more we begin to move away from the depth and vastness of life, and also, from our own inner self and our true purpose and goal. Then all that matters is holding on to individual beliefs, competing for them, and fighting for them, which incidentally feed the ego and give rise to many insecurities and arrogance because our sense of the self, our identity, and our confidence is now derived from these beliefs, concepts, and labels.

Ego, which often likes to operate in a bubble, easily identifies with all things material and keeps us trapped in beliefs, concepts, and labels connected to the material, such as our appearance, name, gender, status, rank, lineage, religion, nationality, etc. And the more materially conscious we are, the less our spiritual orientation becomes. Meaning, the more material consciousness or ego consciousness increases, the more we begin to operate through our unnatural state. Our limited mindset makes us operate through limiting beliefs that build excessive attachment with all that is temporary and ever changeable or unpredictable, resulting in insecurity, greed, anger, arrogance, jealousy, attachments, and tendencies that are the byproduct of the ego.

Simply put, when the consciousness identifies too much with the physical form, it makes one see the self as no different from the body, one's name, status, designation, relationships, social image, etc. And till the time these factors remain stable in life, one remains at ease or rather happy and peaceful with the self. Because in such a scenario, one tends to feel good about the self! But the moment there is any negative shift or any kind of disorder in these aspects, one becomes turbulent because now, one's problems are not anywhere outside but with the self. So, the fear of losing out on any of these aspects, in any way for that matter, amounts to losing out on the self or feeling a little less about the self. Because now the self is no different from these external factors of life such as one's achievements, labels, social standing, and physical appearance. In such a state, one struggles to hold on to that which is not meant to last forever and it is due to this struggle and fear that too many negative tendencies come into play within our soul personality.

Therefore, the more consciousness identifies with the body or the material aspects, the more a soul remains in its unnatural state. Meaning, that it is more likely to operate through tendencies that exhaust its powers, which otherwise, would flourish in a soul's natural state. And because the egoist self is the temporary acquired self and the opposite of a soul's true self or natural self, it is bound to result in a more pronounced material consciousness. Also, when a soul gets too identified with the body or the ego, it creates a natural conflict within itself. This is because subconsciously, while it wants to operate through its natural state, the ego and mind pull the soul in a direction which is entirely the opposite.

Hence, we can see how with excessive identification with the material, a soul shifts from its spiritual state and the consciousness is drawn to believe that one is the body therefore, everything connected to the body or the world of forms becomes all-important. In fact, a soul can get so deeply involved with its human form that the consciousness as well as the mind start believing the physical aspect as the only reality.

Consequently, staying in its natural state becomes a struggle for a soul and soon, its ego consciousness or the material consciousness starts directing its choices, its ways, its behaviour and most importantly, its complete personality.

And even though our natural state and tendencies do remain, yet, owing to a shift in consciousness, they tend to emerge only fleetingly, leading to a diminishing spiritual sense. So, this is precisely the reason why it is exceedingly important what the consciousness chooses to identify with.

Another important thing to understand here is that body or ego consciousness equals to the unnatural state of a soul because a soul cannot operate out of it for too long. So, when a soul's powers are lost due to excessive identification with the self as the body, when excessive anger, attachments, fear, jealousy, and hatred destroy its inner equilibrium and harmony, there comes a point where it is bound to seek the true self. A point, where it is likely to ask the question, 'Who am I?'

It is then that a soul may go in search of its true self, simply because, being dictated by the ego and living in fear or dealing with anger for too long can easily push the soul to the edge of insanity. In such a scenario, the soul would feel so powerless and restless that it would be compelled to search for the deeper truth.

The fact is that a soul can only be comfortable when it is in its natural environment or natural state or when its natural state is more operative compared to the unnatural. Though when a soul journeys through a world of forms, the consciousness does tend to shift from the spiritual to the ego or the material. But the thing that is imperative in order to maintain the sanity of a soul or the balance within a soul is that its consciousness should be conditioned more spiritually than materially. Therefore, in any given life, what is vital for a soul is to work towards restoring its natural state by operating in life through spiritual consciousness.

Chapter 29

FREQUENCY, VIBRATIONS, AND CONSCIOUSNESS

To understand how we can raise our consciousness and operate through our spiritual nature, we need to understand frequency and vibration. These are two important aspects when it comes to understanding our spiritual reality or how we really are as souls. In short, even though we may never be able to touch or see a soul or know what it looks like, we definitely can figure out its power and decipher some of its characteristics through the frequency it is tuned into and the vibration it generates within its immediate environment.

Being souls or energy beings, we are constantly vibrating at a certain frequency, and it is our vibration that creates our physical, emotional, and experiential reality. Our vibration attracts people, situations, events, and even a specific destiny or life path. So, let's further understand these two important aspects that play a crucial role in creating our state of consciousness.

Soul Frequency

As stated earlier, we are all energy beings, and we use this energy to express, create, and manifest. This energy vibrates at a certain frequency and travels at a certain speed. But the most relevant thing here is the fact that the advancement or evolution of a soul or the state of its consciousness can be determined by the frequency at which it vibrates.

And what are the factors that set a soul's frequency? They are:

1. Habitual patterns of behaviour
2. Preferred ways of responding to life
3. Tendencies stored in its subconscious memory

Depending on these factors, every soul attains a certain frequency. And the more positive and uncomplicated these factors, the higher will be the soul frequency. And the higher a soul's frequency, the more evolved or advanced will be its state of consciousness. As a result, its vibrations will be more powerful and energising.

And so, the reason why more evolved souls vibrate at a higher frequency is because they operate through their natural state and do not deplete their energy by remaining mentally and emotionally invested in ordinary situations, problems, chaos, and the commotion of life. They have the ability to go past the tricks of the ego and resolve any negativity very quickly. This way, they do not absorb the darkness or heaviness of any situation and remain free from getting tangled up. Here's an example to understand this better.

Let's assume that there are two travellers who are going to the same destination. One of them opts to travel by plane and the other by road. So, while the latter is likely to get stuck in traffic jams and roadblocks and thus, his overall progress will be slower, the former will be able to avoid all this trouble by flying directly to his destination in no time.

Now, we can take the same analogy and apply it to two souls journeying on this material plane to reach the same end goal or destination. Among the two souls, the one with a higher frequency, i.e., the one who is way above the complexities, confusions, chaos, and commotion of life and can see things from a broader perspective will definitely journey smoothly and reach the destination faster. Such a soul would be able to travel at a good speed and in hassle-free conditions as they won't be consumed by mundane problems and draining circumstances.

However, this won't be the case with a soul vibrating at a lower frequency as they are very likely to get caught up in worldly entrapments. The journey of such souls will be somewhat difficult, tiring, and of course, time-consuming.

Thus, we can see how the frequency or vibration of a soul creates his or her reality. This phenomenon explains the case of wise men and great mystics and spiritual masters of the past. As is evident, they all chose the higher route or higher frequency to travel through their human journey and which is why they not only successfully achieved enlightenment and liberation from karmic bondage but also delivered the necessary wisdom to the world that even today continues to inspire people.

Owing to their higher vibration, these masters and mystics were able to attract a reality that was pure and powerful and imbibe the necessary knowledge or wisdom which created detachment, freedom, inner power, and peace. Their choice and efforts to attain a higher frequency helped them reach enlightenment and liberation much faster, which are the two most significant goals for every soul on this human journey.

Relationships and Frequency

When we meet someone, our respective energies or vibrating frequencies interact, and it is this interplay of energy that determines whether we are drawn to or repelled by certain people. Another important fact that we must also acknowledge is that there are all sorts of souls on this planet. There are souls who operate through a higher frequency and have positive vibrations and there are also souls with heavy or negative vibrations, owing to the fact that they have opted for a lower frequency. Hence, when two souls who are at different frequencies interact, their vibrations often clash. And when two souls, who are on a similar frequency, interact, their vibrations harmonise, i.e., they get along well!

It is also natural for souls at a lower frequency to be drawn to souls that vibrate at a higher frequency. This happens because souls who have higher consciousness and are more spiritually aligned provide an extremely comforting and nurturing atmosphere which attracts the low-frequency souls who are seeking relief from the tension and chaos within. Though the same happens only with self-awareness, i.e., when souls at a lower frequency are conscious of their state and are willing to change.

So, we see how significant the role of our energies and frequencies is when it comes to our relationships. Unfortunately, there are times, when two people fail to build a rapport or even understand the problem between them as their frequencies do not align. They can be together and yet remain incapable of forming a close bond. However, if the frequencies of two souls match, then it does not take much for them to get along and sustain a relationship. In each other's company, they feel connected and comfortable. Therefore, in the context of relationships, frequency and vibration is something that needs a great amount of attention as well as understanding.

Soul Frequency and Consciousness

Another significant aspect of soul frequency and vibration is that it nudges the consciousness to identify either with the physical or the spiritual. And depending on this identification, a soul's tendencies develop. So, if the frequency of a soul drives the consciousness to identify heavily with physical forms, then tendencies like fear, anger, jealousy, hate, and apathy develop. On the other hand, if the soul frequency makes consciousness identify with the spiritual or at least, a balance of the material (physical) and spiritual, then more peace, happiness, harmony, and power is experienced.

Therefore, the way a soul's personality shapes up depends upon what goes on at the frequency level. So, if a soul at a lower frequency, at any point, desires to raise its consciousness, it will first need to change the frequency at which it is operating. This is the only way to achieve a higher version of the self and improve one's personality, tendencies, consciousness, and reality. Also, some souls are able to progress faster than others, owing to their greater self-awareness and inner strength, and most importantly, because they choose to vibrate at a higher frequency. In other words, they choose to go about life more intelligently and consciously and remain tuned to a more positive, uncomplicated, and elevated soul path.

To summarise, the ultimate aim of all souls on this human journey is to raise their consciousness and by doing so, seek freedom from karmic bondage, acquired tendencies, desires, and sins in order to achieve spiritual growth and ascension. This is the very reason why a soul chooses a human life! Though how a soul eventually progresses towards its goal depends entirely on the frequency it is tuned to as well as the consciousness this frequency creates.

Chapter 30

100 CLUES TO HIGH-FREQUENCY SOULS

Here is an extensive list that showcases tendencies or patterns that high-frequency souls are more likely to exhibit. You can examine yourself or anyone else closely and see how many of these tendencies, behavioural patterns, and preferred ways are more pronounced in you or anyone that you wish to understand as a high-frequency soul.

If your observation and understanding reveal that one has fifty to sixty per cent of these traits, then such an individual can be easily assumed to be an individual who is progressing on his or her evolutionary path. The remaining gap, of course, can be bridged by living more consciously and practising greater self-awareness.

And if any person has seventy-five per cent or more of these traits, then they can be classified as a high-frequency soul. As for the souls below the fifty per cent bracket, they will qualify as people at a lower frequency level.

So, let us understand and decipher how actually do high-frequency souls function.

Tendencies of High-Frequency Souls

1. Truly constructive
2. Independent, yet, collaborative

3. Exemplify goodness
4. Stay willfully unbounded
5. Realists
6. Naturally wise
7. Sacrificing in nature
8. Extremely humble
9. Easily satisfied
10. Have a sharper intellect and a deeper understanding of life
11. Not obsessed with material acquisitions
12. Thrive in simplicity
13. See things as possible
14. Appreciate more
15. Eternal optimists
16. Keen listeners and observers
17. Largely happy
18. Easygoing
19. Always grateful
20. Spirited and enthusiastic
21. Feel fortunate
22. Driven by generosity
23. Easily moved to compassion
24. Sensitive but not overly emotional
25. Unperturbed by those unkind to them
26. Unruffled in turbulent times
27. Show higher endurance to pain
28. Rarely complain
29. Rarely insecure
30. Take life as it comes

31. Think of the greater good
32. Stay effortlessly light-hearted
33. Do not form opinions too soon
34. Do not give up so easily
35. Do not identify with success or failure
36. Do not identify with labels and positions/ designations
37. Like to be on time and hate to keep others waiting
38. Are not in a transactional equation with God
39. Refrain from talking poorly of others
40. Encourage positivity in thoughts, words, and actions
41. Avoid discussing negative information
42. Truthful
43. Love soul-searching
44. Accept what is
45. Do not dwell on the past
46. Focused on goodness more than success
47. Generous with appreciation
48. Flexible to change
49. Choose empathy over judgement
50. Stay self-aware
51. Understand how everything happens for a reason connected to our inner growth
52. Do not get emotionally entangled in other people's stories
53. Trust life
54. Do more than they say
55. Neutral to praise and criticism
56. Do not hold on to hurt or regrets

57. Selfless givers
58. Have wisdom that exceeds their intelligence
59. Make everyone feel good about themselves
60. Have healthy self-belief
61. Seek character building more than fame
62. Seek satisfaction more than appreciation
63. Seek happiness more than excitement
64. Seek inspiration more than gains
65. Seek friendship more than network
66. Seek humility more than power
67. Agreeable with jokes on the self
68. See solitude as necessary
69. Can concentrate
70. Do not use other people's company to vent
71. Hate gossip/small talk
72. Speak their mind
73. Balance work with self-nourishment and pleasure
74. Sidestep the rat race
75. Don't always do things for personal benefits
76. Stay honest in relationships
77. Don't subscribe to conventions/belief systems
78. Not too religious but karma conscious
79. Fearless
80. More progressive than the rest
81. Think ahead of their times
82. Bring a sense of newness to their environment
83. Enjoy nature more than concrete structures
84. Like to participate in regular home chores

85. Devote time to hobbies
86. Passionate about their choices
87. Problem solvers
88. Free thinkers
89. Secret keepers
90. Principled people with strong ethics
91. Intuitive and insightful
92. Influence a healthy change in others
93. Have an energising presence
94. Focus on inner growth
95. Feel empowered by silence
96. Drawn to self-discovery
97. Live in the now
98. Stay ever in pursuit of their higher self
99. Understand death as a transition
100. Cherish everything about life

Chapter 31

100 CLUES TO LOW-FREQUENCY SOULS

Next is an assortment of clues that help identify and understand low-frequency souls. Again, in light of the points mentioned below, you can examine the self or anyone else closely and understand whether or not these traits fit.

If they seem to embody fifty to sixty per cent of the tendencies given below, then it can be concluded that such souls are borderline low-frequency souls. A higher percentage than this would confirm a low-frequency soul. But if a person has less than twenty-five per cent of the given qualities and patterns then he or she is in a safe zone. This person also has greater chances of transitioning to a high-frequency scale.

Given below are the most prominent depleting and damaging patterns and tendencies that emerge while operating at a low frequency.

Tendencies of Low-Frequency Souls

1. See life as an ordeal
2. Believe they are victims in most situations
3. Cannot stop blaming others
4. Talk a lot
5. Criticise a lot

6. Are moody and temperamental
7. Make too much fuss about little things
8. Are easily judgmental
9. Can be cynical and sceptical
10. Over analytical
11. Hard to understand
12. Highly impressionable
13. Have a constant commentary in their heads
14. Remain ever worried about the future
15. Cannot handle crisis
16. Crumble under pressure
17. Have self-inflicted doubts and worries
18. Volatile
19. Rarely live in the moment
20. Reflect a lot on the past
21. Drawn to negative information
22. Like to reflect on what is negative for longer
23. More interested in other people's lives
24. Easily absorb negativity
25. Like to discuss sensational day-to-day stuff
26. Love gossip and small talk
27. Get vicarious pleasure from seeing others suffer
28. Believe in caste, creed, and communities
29. Territorial
30. Easily mentally and physically exhausted
31. Perpetually stressed
32. Deeply insecure
33. Fickle-minded

34. Like to go with popular beliefs/choices
35. Afraid of taking risks
36. Quick to react
37. Give a lot of importance to societal compliance
38. Self-obsessed
39. Stubborn
40. Impulsive
41. Dominating
42. Argumentative
43. Narcissistic
44. Procrastinators
45. Always need to prove their point
46. Always in pursuit of material gains
47. Evaluate the self through material success
48. Have trust issues
49. Low on self-esteem
50. Get easily offended
51. Have trouble concentrating
52. Hate to be alone
53. Anger prone
54. Constant opinion seekers
55. Fearful of being criticised and can't handle criticism
56. Seek self-importance
57. Succumb to praise and flattery
58. Pretentious and image-conscious
59. Take others too seriously
60. Like being ahead of others
61. Thrive in comparison
62. Expect a lot from others

63. Easily jealous
64. Extremists
65. Obsessively pursue sensory comforts and pleasures
66. Stingy givers
67. Restless and edgy
68. Easily provoked
69. Hold on to hurt
70. Accumulate pain
71. Emotionally turbulent
72. Find it hard to own up to mistakes and tender an apology
73. Fear or blame God for life's situations
74. Deeply superstitious and ritualistic
75. Attracted to the razzle-dazzle of the world
76. Identify everything through labels
77. Power, rank, and status driven
78. Definite hoarders
79. Possessive about people and things
80. Have unhealthy attachments in relationships
81. Less empathetic
82. Find charity unnecessary
83. Too self-indulgent
84. Not hesitant in being unscrupulous
85. Easily bored
86. Love to exaggerate
87. Fearful of death
88. Never satisfied
89. Have a fear of failure and loss
90. Hard to please

91. Too defensive about the self
92. More attentive to what's lacking in life and in others
93. Inclined to self-pity
94. Like keeping their mind busy all the time
95. Do not believe in introspection
96. Find silence unnerving
97. Find wisdom unnecessary and boring
98. Ego driven
99. Enjoy artificial environments more than nature
100. Cannot fathom a reality beyond their current form

Chapter 32

HOW TO PLAY OUR ROLE WELL

As human beings, we are blessed with both the power of intuition and the power of intellect, which we can use wisely in order to play our present-life role sensibly, comfortably, and correctly. An important point here is that there are certain key factors that we need to take into consideration in our endeavour to play our role well. These factors can help us create a beautiful harmony between the soul and its role as well as lay a solid foundation to harness the right energy and approach for any given role. Thus, understanding and implementing these key factors are somewhere imperative for every soul.

These factors become more important in light of the fact that today, the challenges posed before us aren't just coming from our own psyche but also the collective consciousness, which is largely driven by physical forms and the ego and that results in negative tendencies such as anger, anxiety, hurt, jealously, greed, etc. And with the spiritual sense staying largely dormant within the realm of individual consciousness, the majority of souls today are vibrating at a low frequency. Also, our unnatural state is increasingly becoming more natural to us, leading to more stress and making the collective energy field not conducive to understanding, accepting, and executing our role accurately.

So, let us explore some of these important factors in detail.

1. **Trust**

As souls, we need to trust our role completely. Regardless of the nature of the role or what it requires us to endure, we need to firmly believe that the role, which has been given to us, is what we one hundred per cent deserve. We need to realise that the role is not just a responsibility but also an opportunity that can help us build inner resources and strength along with a greater balance of the mind and intellect.

By trusting life and the entire process, we generate positive energy and if we keep pumping this energy into our role, we are more than likely to make things easier for us in terms of playing the role successfully. On the contrary, if we are always complaining about our role or feeling unsure, then we just end up creating a whole lot of negativity within. This prevents us from making the most of our role as nothing positive can come through a negative attitude. In other words, the eventual outcome of our assigned role would be the same as our attitude towards it.

Also, trust here not just amounts to positivity towards the role but also positivity towards the self, as how we think about our role is what we eventually become. Therefore, we need to place our complete trust in the role given to us and constantly tell ourselves that our role is meant for our growth and evolution.

An interesting aspect to note here is that the deepest and closest relationship that we have on this human journey is with our role. It is the only relationship that stays with us from the beginning till the very end. And as we all know, there is no relationship in this world which can thrive without trust. Therefore, if we intend to create a successful relationship with our role, we have to live with the belief that the part we are playing best suits our capacity and compliments our interests and that it is the best role for our growth and advancement, it has everything to help us emerge successful and satisfied in life, and there is no one better who can play this role more effectively and efficiently.

So, trust is indeed the foremost thing that a given role needs, for the one who trusts ends up tackling his or her role with love, care, hope, enthusiasm, joy, and commitment. While the one who lacks trust eventually deals with the same role with bitterness, uncertainty, lethargy, confusion, and despair. Also, the one who trusts comes out as a better person as with trust within, one develops a more positive set of tendencies as opposed to when we lack trust. This is because when one harbours only negativity and doubt, one not just dishonours the given role but also dishonours one's own ability to handle the role well.

2. **Attention**

Once we have established trust in the role given to us, we then need to start paying the necessary attention to the role as well as to the self in order to advance on our journey. Paying the necessary attention amounts to investigating the role as well as assessing the self honestly. This, in turn, will help us to know the self better and figure out the gaps or shortcomings that prevent us from playing our role comfortably and correctly. As only by paying the necessary attention can we successfully trace the complexities of our behaviour and personality. Complexities which emerge through acquired tendencies, as opposed to natural ones.

Another reason why honest and sincere attention to one's inner reality is significant is because it not only generates a great amount of self-awareness but also makes the process of inner transformation and growth quite easy. Also, giving attention to the self helps hold on to awareness, which easily comes and goes. And the greater one's self-awareness, the greater are one's chances of switching frequencies from lower to higher and altering consciousness as a result. Paying attention also results in living consciously which is the most crucial thing for a soul's success and its ultimate growth and evolution in this human form.

Thus, we need to focus on our role and the self in our daily life with the intention of making changes from time to time as and when they seem necessary. And by making the necessary effort to understand one's role better and grasp how different it really is from one's soul personality, we can develop our personality and excel in life. Also, with time and enough attention, we would become more adept at intuitively grasping the ways by which our role intends to influence a change in order to help us progress.

3. Surrender

One of the best ways to excel in a particular role is through complete surrender! But what does this phrase imply? Complete surrender means a lot of things such as:

- Accepting everything that our role brings our way without complaining
- Being present to what is and not labelling it as good or bad
- Showing no resistance in case our role demands us to change and adapt
- Staying non-judgmental towards the role and towards one's own ability to play the role well
- Accepting one's need for growth and constantly and keenly learning while playing a certain role

Even though the energy of surrender is empowering, for many of us, questions such as 'Why me?', 'What wrong have I done?', and 'What did I do to deserve this life?' can pose a major hindrance when it comes to surrendering. And what we need to understand here is that such questions create the energy of rejection and doubt, which not only harms the self but also the prospects of our role. It creates stiff resistance towards our assigned role and makes us incapable of using our free will to successfully honour the role's true mandate. Not only that, but such questions also prevent us from learning, growing, and being comfortable with our role and tend to make our energy heavy. Thus, a lack of surrendering attitude can truly stagnate any soul and even depreciate its existing powers.

Questions around our role also reflect our unwillingness to cooperate with the divine mandate, which only gets revealed to us through our role. And so, when we question this mandate, it is liable to make us weaker as souls. An important point that we need to understand is that such questions arise from our ego which often tends to misguide us. It either makes us feel like a victim or believe that we are right and so, there is no need to change anything about the self. Ego also doesn't let us be present to what is and makes us want to escape reality.

In a nutshell, a lack of surrender means being in conflict with life and rejecting it completely which includes its teachings and experiences that are meant to help us progress as a soul. For in case of conflict, all we do is fight—fight with the self, with life, situations, experiences, destiny, and people—and in the process, we waste time struggling and not learning or improving.

On the other hand, surrendering means to accept life in its totality. It reflects a beautiful harmony as well as shows a positive intent and a deep desire to understand, learn, absorb, enjoy, and grow through the role given to us. And through surrendering, we acknowledge our higher purpose. Through surrendering, we show a willingness to undertake this journey for the sake of our own evolution. And it is this positive attitude coupled with active wisdom that unveils the abundant blessings of life.

4. Simplicity

While we may think our energy or our approach matters little in life, in truth, it is what makes all the difference when it comes to success or failure in a given role. We need to remain careful about the way our mind and intellect function because if we have a tendency to overcomplicate our thoughts and our energy, we are more than likely to blunder in our assigned role.

Thus, it is important to not let the mind get entangled in too much analysis and just go with the flow of events and experiences that are integral to any role. We need to absorb what our role is attempting to teach us through the events and experiences of our life and allow the same to inspire a more positive set of tendencies within us. We need to enjoy the role along with all the changes that it brings about.

And we can achieve this by nurturing the energy of acceptance, flexibility, and purity, which, in turn, originates from the simplicity of the mind and intellect. This is because when one's mind and intellect do not complicate a role by overthinking, over-analysing, or over-evaluating, our role goes about unhindered. Because now, there are no blockages in our own energy that would otherwise tend to complicate our role and make us stagnate. Here, we don't resist learning from our role and allow it to flow seamlessly. Thus, we can see why simplicity is one of the most essential factors for the successful handling of any role.

The simplicity of the mind and the intellect not only reflects the purity of the soul but also its inherent strength to honour a role. This simplicity also sends out positive energy and intent which the universe always reciprocates and returns to us in a more amplified and intensified manner. Therefore, when we approach our role with simplicity, the universe is more than likely to simplify the events, experiences, situations, and circumstances of our life or in other words, we are likely to attract the same. This is because the energy that comes back to us is the energy that we send out. And it is this energy which touches others as a vibration and influences their response towards us. Meaning, the response that we are likely to get will be dictated by the vibes we put out. And our inherent simplicity ensures that our energy stays light and our vibe remains uncomplicated and powerful.

On the contrary, people who are always overthinking and over-analysing tend to not grow as much. They complicate their energy, which, in turn, complicates various aspects of their lives. Such people create their own obstacles and remain ever stuck in resolving their inner mess instead of creating a harmonious balance in their individual personalities. On top of that, the confusion and stress generated from their constant thinking further dampen their chances of success in life.

By contrast, people who just go with the flow of life and think little or those who have fairly simple thoughts surrounding their role tend to go about their role in a smooth fashion. They neither complicate their own energy nor what they get in return as experiences and events.

5. Intelligence

Intelligence is again an important factor when it comes to progressing on our journey as a soul and essaying our role. But what is true intelligence?

- True intelligence is in understanding what works for us and what does not.
- It is in doing what is right and what is needed in order to be successful in our given role.
- It is about playing our role in a way that makes us worthy of success and divine help.

- It is in understanding that while facing the challenges of our given role through calmness and maturity, we can avoid suffering.
- It is in nurturing patience, fortitude, and greater willpower, which help us earn the rewards of grace.
- It lies in realising that this is just a role and that it is temporary and not something that will continue forever.
- It aligns us with the divine will, which, in turn, becomes our strength and power.

And any soul that builds and operates through such intelligence is bound to play its role successfully. For true intelligence not just elevates us as souls but also helps us vibrate at a higher frequency.

6. Gratitude

Gratitude for our role and for life, in general, is by far the most essential factor that can help us excel.

And real gratitude begins with positive intent, which transforms into positive energy, and it is this energy that gets rewarded in due course of time. So, when we express gratitude towards our role or when we simply sit and reflect on how valuable this opportunity is to learn, express, feel, touch, and see life as well as everything connected to it, we create harmony and joy within. This makes us operate through higher consciousness and makes it easy for us to essay our role well. On the contrary, when we are ungrateful or ignorant of the immense power and value of our role, then we naturally become negative, unhappy, and critical. This also makes us indulge in unhealthy comparisons with others and show frivolousness towards our own individual roles. Such heavy and dark emotions pull us down to a far lower state, where our consciousness becomes disempowered and clouded. And once in such a state, we can continue thinking and feeling miserable and keep struggling in our given role, till a rude awakening hits us.

An important thing to remember is that gratitude is not just feeling thankful for whatever good one has, it is also accepting what is not good and being okay with it. For true gratitude is in accepting life as a whole, not just the bits and pieces.

Also important is the understanding that gratitude doesn't mean uttering some words for the sake of it. Rather, it is deep underlying feelings of love and appreciation for our role, which sometimes, does not even need any words. It is a conscious realisation of being benefited by the role assigned to us, coupled with an intent to learn and advance even more through the role. In fact, gratitude and learning have a mutual connection as when we are able to learn and evolve through our role, we are bound to feel a sense of gratitude towards the role for helping us mature and progress as a being. And when such an emotion of gratefulness takes over our consciousness, we feel inspired and fulfilled. This positive and powerful state of consciousness tends to attract more power and positivity, which helps us play our role more effectively.

7. Visualise

As much as possible, one must attempt to visualise one's given role with positive imagination and constructive thoughts and ideas. This is important because our imagination or thoughts are more powerful than our words. They carry a certain energy, which, though not obvious, is extremely creative and nourishing.

The reason why our positive thoughts and imagination amount to positive reinforcement is because our energy flows wherever our attention goes and that aspect of life grows. Therefore, when we visualise our role with powerful and positive imagination, our energy flows in that direction and sooner or later, the same manifests as our reality.

Thus, we can see that our thoughts and imagination have immense power and can influence both internal as well as external reality. However, we must remember that while we are visualising, there must not be any desire in us because it carries with it the energy of lack which is negative and can act as a hindrance in manifesting positive results.

8. Harmonise

Harmony leads to a peaceful and powerful union between the soul and its role. So, in order to play our role well, we need to harmonise with it and embrace it wholeheartedly. Let's explore this further.

Harmony is important because it creates the energy of peace, acceptance, respect, love, care, and devotion, and the same is likely to help us and our role thrive and blossom with joy and beauty. Harmony also means that we must not complain about our role as too much negative chatter around one's role tends to complicate one's own life, experiences, and circumstances. It can even bring stagnation and hinder our growth. For complaining is again a battle of sorts, where a soul tends to create anxiety, heaviness, darkness, and unhappiness around its role. This not only blocks the soul's path but also attracts similar energy, which further complicates one's role.

So, if we want to play our role well, then complaining must be replaced with harmony. And harmony includes positive affirmations and constructive thoughts, words, feelings, and emotions showing gratitude, love, and respect for the role, regardless of how easy or difficult it may be. An important point regarding loving and accepting our roles is that it not just amounts to honouring life but also helps us settle our karmic debts. These debts, if not settled, impede our progress and add more confusion to our outlook as well as to our understanding of life.

One also needs to remember that every individual's role is designed and customised as per their soul personality and the accumulated karmic debts of that person. Hence, each and every role gives the individual a chance to enhance his or her own personality and also settle their karmic debts. This also implies that paying attention to someone else's role and being ignorant or unhappy with one's own is purely a waste of time and opportunity to free the self from the karmic burden. As only by harmonising with our role can we successfully settle karma and grow as a soul.

9. Accept Transience

To understand this point, let's first understand that:

- We are all travellers on this planet and nothing lasts forever, neither the difficulties of our role nor the rewards and pleasure.
- Every role has a finite time frame and purpose.
- We take a role to fulfil a specific purpose but in a fixed period.

These are some universal truths which show us the importance of reminding ourselves, time and time again, that who we are and what we are experiencing is only for a short while. And therefore, in this limited time, we need to focus on overcoming all challenges that hinder us from playing our role to the best of our ability and not waste time feeling stressed, confused, or lost.

This aspect is similar to going to a shopping store or a supermarket with a list of items to purchase. We know that we have limited time to do the needful, so we do not waste time thinking about anything worrisome or idling away time in careless thinking or talking. Rather, we just do what needs to be done without wasting a minute, so that in the end, we not just accomplish what we came to do but also feel good about what we managed to put together in this fixed time.

That is precisely how our role needs to be dealt with. Remembering the finality of our role would not just shake us out of any carelessness but also inspire and push us to do our best. And this is exceedingly important because even though our roles are temporary, what does stay and become an integral part of our soul memory is how we felt while dealing with a role. This is because that memory gets recorded as a tendency, which stays with the soul and becomes the very basis of who we are. So, it can be happiness or sadness, peace or anxiety, fear or courage and power, or humility or arrogance. Thus, whatever the tendency, it remains and goes with the soul.

10. Witness

It is important to be a witness or an observer to one's role, rather than making the role one's very identity. For doing the latter amounts to being attached to the role and drifting away from our main purpose, which is self-improvement through the role. This also means that we neither do justice to the role nor to the reason why the role was assigned to us. But when we see a clear difference between the self and the role and take the role as just a means to an end and not as something final, we achieve what's necessary.

Also, when we assume that the role is who we are, we lose connection with our true self and operate more out of ego. For it is the ego that misleads us and makes us identify with labels. This way, we neither pursue our role correctly nor are we able to progress and develop the self through the role.

However, by being a witness or an observer to our role, we are able to create a space between the self and the role. This helps us to consciously differentiate between the role and the self (soul) and it is this differentiation, which not just sets us free of worries and fears but also enables us to understand the accurate demands of our role and our own psychological and emotional state while responding to the demands of the role. Any such understanding is important for our growth and evolution.

Being a witness to our role also makes us aware that the role is a wonderful means to make the self better as well as a means of getting involved with people and the world. This allows us to see the role quite dispassionately and prevents us from getting too attached to the role and creating self-worth on the basis of our role, which can easily mislead us and harm our self-esteem and inner peace. On the other hand, by being a witness, we remain secure and focused. It also allows us to be involved in a more constructive manner as it makes us understand that we have nothing to lose in the process and all we can do is give our best.

Therefore, being a witness to our role empowers us, makes us think and act independently, and helps us invest our time and attention in doing what is necessary rather than just trying to forcefully fit into and embody our assigned role.

11. Unlearn and Learn

By coming into this world and taking up a human role, a soul sets itself up for a lot of learning. This is the very objective of every role assigned to a soul. And the reason why we are all here to learn is that only through learning can we grow, mature, and graduate to the next level. Because when we learn, we understand the self better and recognise our flaws and shortcomings, and only then can we bring about the necessary change.

If we observe closely, this change implies replacing what is not right in us with something better in order to improve ourselves. In other words, we would be required to unlearn things before we can learn new things or more precisely put, one can only learn after one has unlearned. And this applies to all aspects of life such as our approach, behaviour, attitude, mindset, conditioning, beliefs, etc.

We can see this phenomenon in action in our day-to-day lives. While playing a role, we tend to drop certain tendencies from our soul personality and gain a few. But if we show resistance to change or if we find the process of unlearning difficult, then there is no room for something new to fit in. This way, a soul neither evolves nor plays its role appropriately. Hence, learning and unlearning are both necessary for soul maturity. For if the old is held too tightly, nothing new can move in or breathe. Also, unlearning is the only way one can alter one's conditioning as it helps clear out the clutter within and removes any blockages that prevent mental, emotional, and spiritual growth. Unlearning also helps break the wheel of karma by letting go of old ways and patterns of behaviour that are often the cause of all karmic complications. Most importantly, unlearning is the only way one can challenge the ego and get rid of it through new learning that leads to new and evolved patterns of thinking and behaviour.

Therefore, we must endeavour to unlearn, as only then, would we be able to learn what we have come to learn through our given role and lifetime. Without unlearning and learning, we cannot give the role what it truly needs and find growth and evolution. Also, having the flexibility and acumen to adapt to what the given role demands is the only way to grow and mature as souls and play our individual roles well.

12. Develop

The best way to play one's role well is by actually playing it well! And the biggest incentive and reward that one can enjoy in this process is one's own progress and growth as an individual and as a soul. Though in order to constantly progress, we need to develop ourselves consistently through a given role. This provides the necessary incentive, encouragement, and motivation to keep moving ahead on our journey.

Therefore, our effort should be to do everything to develop the self through our individual roles. After all, the purpose of our role is to help us develop into finer beings and the more we take the role as a means to grow our own personality and behaviour and develop ourselves mentally, emotionally, and psychologically, the more we are likely to do justice to a given role. For the purpose of our role is not just to fulfil a set of duties, responsibilities, tasks, and physical activities but also to remove our own deficiencies in our personality and behaviour.

After all, we are all here to become better. We are here to progress as souls by developing the right set of tendencies and a balanced inner personality. We are here to raise our consciousness and become purer souls with a greater sense of happiness, peace, and power within. And the only way we can achieve this sense of completeness and inner bliss is by embracing the necessary change that a role is likely to influence upon our soul personality. A change which comes by surrendering to the most fundamental demands of a given role and by being flexible towards altering and improving the self to best suit our current role. And this change is crucial to develop through a given role.

Also, change or inner transformation can only take place when we master the art of being and through it, become a new and better person. And regardless of how challenging it may be, the way we can bring about this change is by incorporating a positive set of tendencies in our lifestyle, behaviour, and attitude.

So, we can conclude that change not only helps us advance as souls but also infuses more power into our being. And embracing such a change or self-transformation assumes the highest value and importance when it comes to playing our role well. For once we start developing as a person through our given role, there is absolutely nothing that can hold us back from emerging stronger, happier, lighter, and purer!

13. Seek wisdom

Wisdom is our guiding light on this journey, and it can help us go beyond any limitations that prevent us from successfully executing our roles. By seeking higher wisdom, we create our path to our higher self and this autonomically helps us give our best to our chosen role.

Most of us, when we come across pearls of wisdom, we immediately feel charged and positive and experience the need to share such wisdom with those close to us because the piece of wisdom elevates us to a more empowering thought process. A thought process that unlocks the doors to self-exploration and brings about a sense of awakening that is imperative to our growth.

The reason why wisdom leads to awakening is that it has the power to melt one's ego and humble the mind. It also has the power to raise intelligence and lead to a more inward-driven, constructive, and elevated thought process, which helps one align with one's higher self. And once we become aware of the ego and our self-awareness increases, we are automatically able to unlock the doors of the mind and bring in the necessary changes that not just help us become better beings but also enable us to play our role well.

Also, if we are not exposed to higher wisdom, we continue living unconsciously and in oblivion. Our growth begins only after getting exposed to higher wisdom, which helps investigate one's current state of being. And only upon such an enquiry can one really know whether one is operating through ego consciousness or not. Also, we become self-aware only when this internal enquiry is initiated, through the help of spiritual knowledge. Self-awareness helps us awaken from our slumber and filter our consciousness to know what is pure and what is not. Something, that's vital to playing our human role effectively.

14. Practise Self-Awareness

Once we are able to create a reasonable amount of self-awareness, it is necessary to constantly put it into practice. It is important to stay aware of the more predominant thoughts and feelings within. Which can range from good to bad, draining to empowering, inspiring to damaging, etc. The important thing is to acknowledge each and every recurring thought, feeling, and emotion and stay aware of what is within us, in terms of both right and wrong. Because only when we are truly conscious of the thoughts and feelings that arise within us can we actually become aware of the tendencies through which we largely operate. And it is this awareness that can further help us to replace the undesirable tendencies and strengthen the good ones, which is essential for playing our role well.

The continuous process of identifying the self, how we think, what we feel, how our emotions play out, and how we take life in all its unpredictability and glory is what makes the greatest difference when it comes to raising our individual consciousness and getting the most out of our role. Here, we need to bear in mind the simple fact that each event, each experience, and each moment playing out in our lives is only a catalyst to a reaction within. And there is always something or the other that the mind and the intellect keep busy thinking, analysing, feeling, responding to, and accumulating. Therefore, it is of utmost importance to remain aware of what really is being processed in the consciousness and what is eventually becoming a part of one's conditioning.

With constant awareness, one lives more consciously and any sort of damaging, self-ignorant, and excessive behaviour eventually gets corrected. As the moment awareness replaces the ignorance within us, we automatically begin to raise our frequency. This helps us get the power to shift consciousness from ordinary to a more refined state, which is bound to help us play our role well.

The more we practice living with self-awareness, the higher our frequency becomes and as a result, consciousness becomes purer and more elevated. And this way, we are able to successfully influence the mind and intellect to choose the right set of thoughts, feelings, and responses. Meaning, we begin to discriminate better, integrate higher wisdom, and positively influence our thoughts and actions. And the more we are able to correct the self at the level of thoughts and feelings, the more our tendencies improve. Our dark, heavy, and negative thoughts, feelings, and behavioural patterns get replaced with lighter and more positive ones, which help us to operate more from the natural tendencies of peace, love, power, and happiness. And once the more complex tendencies of anger, ego, hurt, pain, jealousy, etc. are replaced, we are likely to remain in our natural state for longer. Here, one also needs to understand that one cannot let go of any unnatural tendencies, unless one starts operating more out of their natural tendencies. The same needs to be used far more, so that what's damaging is drained out.

Now let us look at what we exactly mean by practising awareness. Practising awareness amounts to watching one's thoughts, acknowledging one's feelings, and observing one's responses or reactions while also understanding and accepting them as they are. And it can be practised in solitude as well as in moments of busyness or when surrounded by people. But in both situations, self-awareness can be practised by momentarily withdrawing from external observation and looking within and paying attention to one's thoughts and feelings. Especially, when confronted by extremes, either heightened excitement and joy or heightened fear and anxiety, practising self-awareness can be very useful.

Also, for awareness to remain, one important thing is to churn wisdom as this helps in keeping self-awareness steady. For what happens is that sometimes we get the realisation or the sense of how we are and what we need to change in the self, but if we do not keep imbibing and assimilating wisdom, our realisation itself fades out and we get on with life with the same inner state that's controlled by the ego.

So, even though practising self-awareness may be an all-consuming and painstaking process and may not even deliver instant results, over a reasonable period of time, we can reach a point where we know the self so well that influencing a change becomes easier. And such a change is always lasting, comfortable, and stable. It is not forced, not achieved through suppression, not short-lived, and not even painful or difficult. Thus, with higher and constant self-awareness, we are able to grow into higher beings and are able to do full justice to our roles.

15. Stillness

Stillness is when one withdraws from the outer world and pays complete attention to their thoughts until they stop after which one experiences inner silence. It can also be likened to being an observer to the self and one's thoughts as when we watch our thoughts, they lose momentum and eventually stop. And even though the duration of this experience may be brief, this pause creates the necessary space between our thoughts. This space energises us, empowers us, and makes us more creative and productive. And without this, no role can be essayed well. Thus, it is important to introduce ourselves to this state of stillness from time to time and preferably, on a daily basis.

As mentioned, even if these moments of stillness last only for a few seconds or minutes, during these precious moments, we can regain inner peace, which automatically transports us to a higher state of being. By practising stillness, we can recharge our mind and energy. This rejuvenation occurs as these moments of stillness give us the necessary break from our random, recurring thoughts which only drain and exhaust us. And it is this sense of rejuvenation or resting of the mind that is likely to bring up new and powerful insights, which are useful for one's mental, spiritual, psychological, and even material growth and also significantly contribute to our creative abilities. But most importantly, it helps us to play our role effectively.

Stillness also brings clarity to our thinking. It helps realign our thought process and see things with greater precision and without a trace of bias. It pulls the mind away from all the noise, from an unnecessary and draining thought process, which most of us are conditioned to think as normal.

However, a mind which is constantly in overdrive not only loses its power to create but also the ability to see things with clarity and accuracy. It is the absence of this very power and ability that often thwarts any kind of self-realisation and positive change for a soul. Thus, when stillness is practised, it nourishes both the mind and the intellect and gives us the desired power to see things with a sense of newness as well as correctness. Something that helps us do full justice to our given mandates and individual roles.

16. Meditative life

Meditation is a good way to bring greater efficacy into the way one plays their respective role. But meditation doesn't amount to just practice. It needs to be a way of life as only then can it help us make a positive difference in the way we play our roles.

A little contrary to popular belief, meditation is beyond mere practice. It is a response to life that comes from one's inner awareness when it is operating through peace, stability, happiness, love, compassion, cheer, empathy, power, confidence, courage and bliss. Basically, a response to life that emerges from one's natural state or one's higher self.

Thus, we can say that meditation is not something we do but rather, it is something we live. The fact is that most times when we are peaceful, detached, and silent within, we are actually meditating. And a habit of consciously living in such a state makes meditation an integral part of our life.

So, when it comes to playing our human role correctly and effectively, meditation can be a great boon, only if instead of just practising meditation, we start living consciously and operating out of peace for as long as we can. For peace is the foundation for the successful execution of any role and without inner peace, the role can neither benefit us nor can we understand and deliver what it requires.

The following points shed light on what true meditation implies:

- Meditation arises from a state of progressive consciousness or a state where we choose to live more attentively and with greater self-awareness, detached from fear, impulses, and expectations.
- Meditation is a complete surrender to what is. It is being present to life at all times and living consciously in the now.

- Meditation is when our inner stability and stillness interact with people and situations. It is when we make peace with the self and this very peace can be felt or experienced by others. In other words, meditation is a state of being, which elevates us and transforms our energy in ways that has a calming and enriching effect on others.
- Meditation is a way of life that originates from inner completeness and balance. It is not a mere act or a duty-bound exercise but a natural way of living life. A way in which there is complete acceptance of life, complete participation along with a whole lot of appreciation for life.
- Meditation is when our inner state becomes independent of our outer environment. It is a constant state of inward attentiveness which frees us from being senselessly driven by worldly encounters or experiences. So, regardless of our outer circumstances, we are able to deal with the same with total equanimity and lack of resistance and inner disturbance. This is only possible to achieve when our inner state stays empowered and neutral to what life brings. Such an unbiased and mature response to life can actually be termed meditation.
- Meditation is an outcome of wisdom, stillness, and self-awareness. It is the fruit of all these activities and it finds expression in our inner harmony. It is a practical manifestation of our positive and natural tendencies.

To conclude, all the aspects covered above make us understand that true meditation is more than what it is largely believed to be. True meditation is a way of life and if we are able to combine a meditative life with our role, we can not only play our role well but derive the most extraordinary results.

CONCLUSION

In the end, we can say we have lived a life well if we have progressed internally. But for that to happen, we need to understand the self, look deeper than what we know of the self, and discover something that will transform the self. And even though it is not that easy or, at times, even unexciting for us to sincerely seek, understand, and learn more about the self with complete honesty and humility to become a higher version of the self, the truth remains that without making such efforts, we really cannot do full justice to this life, which is a precious opportunity to bring about growth and evolution for each and every soul.

As individuals, we do not know how long it took for us to earn this one life. We also cannot even comprehend what it took to reach this point in our journey. But what we can definitely relate to is how we are as a person, as a soul. Therefore, in this given life, we can at least try to know our own truth, attempt to become better and wiser, and make our light shine brighter.

What we need to realise is that though the world around us may be transient, everything in life may be temporary, and we cannot even predict how long we will remain in a human form, amid all the question marks and uncertainty, what we do know is that we will be with the self forever. We will continue as energy beings, as souls, regardless of our human existential reality.

So, whether or not we have this life on earth, we will always operate through our tendencies, our soul personality. And so, the only thing we have control over is the amalgamation of tendencies that each one of us holds inside or outside of this human journey. Thus, it becomes our prerogative to improve the self and our tendencies to become more peaceful, powerful, blissful, and free. Simply put, we are here to become higher beings. This is our sole purpose and the primary reason why we are here. So, we must make every possible effort to know the self, work on the self, better the self, and liberate the self from the ego. Ego which leads to desires, doubts, dilemmas, attachments, delusions, fears, falsehoods, and everything that desiccates our power to exist peacefully and joyfully.

Remember that for as long as we live, we have the means to create a self-sufficient state of the being and if we, as souls, can evolve to this wonderful state in our human form, then we would have lived this life extremely well. But for the same to happen, we must begin from somewhere and that is by first asking—Why we are who we are?

ACKNOWLEDGEMENTS

This book resulted from almost a decade invested in observing and understanding human behaviour, habits, and personality types. It came from listening and connecting with people, their stories, and their way of life and by putting the pieces of their individual puzzles together. And all this happened while I was on my own journey to self-discovery and growth. It was as though the universe was teaching me about myself through others and was helping me evolve and mature.

I realised there was no better way to learn than by reflecting on other people's journeys and what they shared with me while I was on the other side as a friend, a listener, a confidante, and a counsellor. It took me some time to connect the dots and go deeper into their lives, their purpose, and the true mandate for which they were here. And two subjects that helped me arrive at logical conclusions were spirituality and astrology. I am ever grateful to the ancient masters and the great rishis, who left behind their precious legacy of wisdom and techniques to help us understand the self and our lives better.

Why We Are Who We Are is a book that wasn't planned or conceived; it happened. It happened due to insights and information shared by people who opened up to me with their truth and put their trust in me to understand their life situations and state of mind. I extend my deepest gratitude and appreciation to all of them. They helped me grow more than any piece of knowledge, a teacher, or a guide. And so, whatever I have learnt and shared in this book comes from them.

I thank Hay House India for their belief in the book and for giving me another opportunity to publish with them. I extend my sincere appreciation to Mr Ashok Chopra, Raghav Khattar, and the entire Hay House team that stays dedicated to publishing books of enormous spiritual value and books with higher meaning that continue to positively transform and enrich people's lives.

This is the second book with my editor, Aditya Jarial, and it has been an absolute joy to work with him. His contribution to this book is invaluable. His sound piece of editorial guidance has helped the book gain depth and develop far more intelligently than the original manuscript. A big aspect of Aditya's work is his sensible and meticulous approach. The effort is there to be seen, and he is spot-on in pointing out the areas of improvement. I thank Aditya for investing his precious time and energy in this project and for patiently helping me polish the book.

Many thanks to my parents, my dear pet, Zeus, and my sister, Swati, for her love and unfailing support, her rock-solid contribution to my journey, my happiness, and my achievements. I am so grateful for her luminous presence in my life as well as her positivity that never ceases to amaze me.

Most of all, I thank my better half and my best friend, Manoj, for being the best advisor and the greatest motivator in my professional journey. I also owe a lot of my personal growth to this wise, nurturing, and generous soul. And I don't have enough words to thank him for his ever-inspiring presence, humour, patience, unconditional support, and constant push that always helps me do better.

I would also like to express my appreciation to my kind and dear friend Lalit.

Lastly, a big thank you to the readers who helped in making my debut book, *Living Spirituality*, a success. Each of your comments humbles and inspires me every day.

'The gateways to wisdom and knowledge are always open.'

Louise Hay